Religious Education in the Mirror of a Life Trajectory

The study of religious education is of great interest in analyzing how schools and educational authorities address the demands of multicultural and multi-religious societies and states. As diversity increases through migration, globalization and conflicts, schools are faced with equally diverse challenges, one of which is the religious and cultural diversity that characterizes schools and communities. While many studies have focused on this change and its impact in politics, school and classrooms, relatively few have focused on how teachers and educators have fared. Sitting between the new policies and school demographics, teachers and educators have shaped the policy in their engagements.

The study of life trajectories shows that the lines between religion and religious education are blurred in personal life histories, and that positions can shift due to personal and contextual developments. They point to the innovative and unexpected turns that individuals trace in their personal life journeys. This book reminds us that we need to pay more attention to the teachers, principals, managers and public intellectuals who shape and are shaped by the changing context of religion and religious education.

This book was originally published as a special issue of *Religion & Education*.

Abdulkader Tayob holds the chair in Islam, Religious Values and Public Life in Africa at the University of Cape Town, South Africa. He has published extensively on Islam in South Africa and modern Muslim intellectuals. Currently, he leads a project on religion education in South Africa that interrogates the history and future of the programme with social scientists, educators and teachers.

Religious Education in the Mirror of a Life Trajectory

Edited by
Abdulkader Tayob

Routledge
Taylor & Francis Group

LONDON AND NEW YORK

First published 2019
by Routledge
2 Park Square, Milton Park, Abingdon, Oxon, OX14 4RN, UK

and by Routledge
52 Vanderbilt Avenue, New York, NY 10017, USA

First issued in paperback 2020

Routledge is an imprint of the Taylor & Francis Group, an informa business

British Library Cataloguing-in-Publication Data
A catalogue record for this book is available from the British Library

ISBN 13: 978-0-367-58475-7 (pbk)
ISBN 13: 978-1-138-33533-2 (hbk)

Typeset in Minion Pro
by codeMantra

Publisher's Note
The publisher accepts responsibility for any inconsistencies that may have arisen during the conversion of this book from journal articles to book chapters, namely the possible inclusion of journal terminology.

Disclaimer
Every effort has been made to contact copyright holders for their permission to reprint material in this book. The publishers would be grateful to hear from any copyright holder who is not here acknowledged and will undertake to rectify any errors or omissions in future editions of this book.

Contents

Citation Information

The chapters in this book were originally published in the journal *Religion & Education*, volume 44, issue 1 (January 2017). When citing this material, please use the original page numbering for each article, as follows:

Chapter 6

Continuity and Change: Experiences of Teaching Religious Education in the Light of a Life Trajectory of Hifz and Secular Education
Jenny Berglund
Religion & Education, volume 44, issue 1 (January 2017) pp. 88–100

Chapter 7

Islamic Modernism and Colonial Education in Northern Nigeria: Na'ibi Sulaiman Wali (1927–2013)
Alexander Thurston
Religion & Education, volume 44, issue 1 (January 2017) pp. 101–117

For any permission-related enquiries please visit:
http://www.tandfonline.com/page/help/permissions

Notes on Contributors

Cok Bakker's educational background is in Theology and Educational Theory. At Utrecht University, the Netherlands he holds the chair for 'Worldview development in a multi-religious context.'

Jenny Berglund is an Associate Professor in the Study of Religions Department at Södertörn University, Huddinge Municipality, Sweden and a Visiting Associate Professor in the Warick Religions and Education Research Unit at the University of Warwick, Coventry, UK.

Joseph Chita obtained an MA in International Education and Development from Oslo and Akershus University College, Norway—Oslo in 2010 and Master of Education in Religious Studies from the University of Zambia, Lusaka, Zambia in 2011. He joined the University of Zambia as a Lecturer in the Department of Religious Studies in 2011.

Liam Gearon is an Associate Professor in the Department of Education and a Senior Research Fellow at Harris Manchester College, University of Oxford, UK. He also holds two honorary professorships in Australia, at the Australian Catholic University, Sydney and at the University of Newcastle, Callaghan. He is an appointed member of both the Arts and Humanities Research Council (AHRC) Peer Review College and the Economic and Social Research Council (ESRC) Peer Review College.

Arniika Kuusisto is a University Lecturer and Docent at the University of Helsinki, Finland, presently on a three-year research leave (2016–2019) with her Academy of Finland-funded research project examining children's value-learning trajectories during transition from Early Childhood Education to primary school.

Garth Mason is a Senior Lecturer in the Department of Religious Studies and Arabic at the University of South Africa, Pretoria, South Africa.

Nelly Mwale is a Lecturer at the University of Zambia, Lusaka, Zambia in the Department of Religious Studies. She holds a Master of Education in Religious Studies (Med (RS)) from the University of Zambia.

Abdulkader Tayob holds the chair in Islam, Religious Values and Public Life in Africa at the University of Cape Town, South Africa.

Ina ter Avest is a psychologist of religion and culture. She is an Emeritus Professor of Religion and Education at Inholland University of Applied Sciences, Hoofddorp, the Netherlands and a former Senior Lecturer at the VU University Amsterdam, the Netherlands.

Alexander Thurston is a Visiting Assistant Professor of African Studies at Georgetown University, Washington, DC, USA.

Wolfram Weisse is a Senior Professor of Religion, Education and Dialogue at the University of Hamburg, Germany. He is the Director of the Academy of World Religions of the University of Hamburg and Coordinator of the European research project 'Religion and Dialogue in Modern Societies.'

Acknowledgement

The conference and publication was supported in part by the National Research Foundation of South Africa (Reference number (UID) 85397). The opinions, findings and conclusions or recommendations expressed are that of the organizers and authors, and the NRF accepts no liability whatsoever in this regard.

Life Trajectories of Educators Between Religion and Religious Education

Abdulkader Tayob

All the world's a stage, And all the men and women merely players. They have their exits and their entrances, And one man in his time plays many parts, His acts being seven ages.

Shakespeare, *As You Like It*, Act 2, Scene 7

Religion education, defined as the teaching about religion in schools, colleges, and universities, is increasingly becoming the norm around the globe. There is wide-spread recognition that students need to be exposed to the many religious traditions and worldviews that they will encounter in their lives. There are very few places on the globe where diverse religious adherents and communities do not share schools, neighborhoods, towns and cities. In this often-bewildering context, knowing and understanding religious symbols and values is becoming an essential part of education.

In this new context, teachers are expected to re-examine their values and traditions, and also their former training in confessional religious education. Many are nurtured and trained in their own specific traditions, but now expected to expose their students to diversity, pluralism, and sometimes conflict among cultural and religious groups. This special volume is focused on the life trajectories and journeys of educators and public intellectuals as they navigate through this changing terrain. The contributors take life trajectories seriously, and shed light on the nature, form, and meaning of education in religions for each individual and in each context. These journeys direct us to the educational, intellectual, and political struggles that religious educators experience over time. They focus on the changes that educators navigate through new policies, increasingly diverse private and public contexts, and their own deep, personal experiences. They include the ensuing tensions but also the creativity that has emerged from this engagement.

This attention to the experiences of life trajectories is useful for the study of religion and religious education. As teachers work with new policies and experience the lived diversity in the classroom, they take different positions on the subject. Some embrace the new models that insist that theology and religious instruction should be left to the home and religious institutions. Others adopt a middle position as they see the value of religion in identity formation. The essays in this volume offer perspectives on how educators adopt and create new directions in religious education, from their personal experiences over a long period of time.

The study of biographies and life trajectories is not new in the study of religions. Inspired by Ricouer's concept of narrative time, some of these studies have focused on the processes of individualization and self-actualization.[1] Buitelaar and Zock brought together a number of studies on religion in self-narratives among immigrants.[2] Life trajectories have been more extensively studied in history, gender studies, and anthropology. Jill Lepore locates the study of life trajectories, which she has called *microhistory*, between biography and history. Whereas biography focuses on the unique life of an individual, usually someone who made a significant contribution to history, microhistory pointed to the significance of a life in the light of general religious, social, or political developments. Microhistory placed the life of an individual within "the culture as a whole;" where the individual life was often an "allegory" of the whole.[3]

Other historians have suggested that life trajectories may be appreciated against cultural life scripts that are embraced or adapted over time. They have followed life trajectories against norms, values, and expectations of the cultural traditions concerned. The cultural life scripts have been found to stand in dynamic relation with individual life trajectories.[4] Bourdieu's concepts of symbolic capital and habitus have found favor among those working with life trajectories.[5] In an interesting study, Costa has applied these concepts for understanding how new languages are acquired by immigrants.[6]

The study of life trajectories, then, has focused attention on the individual within a larger social or cultural canvass. Individual life trajectories are fascinating for the experience they share about themselves, and for their part in a larger movement and tradition in the culture. Life trajectories have been put in the foreground, without losing sight of the context in which they have embarked on their journeys. The articles in this collection situate the biographies and trajectories of educators between their unique personal journeys, and the larger canvasses of religious and religion education. They offer a rich understanding of critical and important turning points in religion and religious education. Their subjects provide insight and commentary on the social and political changes from which religion and religious education cannot be extricated.

This volume consists of four essays on schools and school systems, and three on educators within the public sphere. Ina ter Avest begins with an essay on two principals in different parts of the Netherlands. She shares the experiences of two pioneers who experimented with a new approach to religion education. Her essay is followed by Mwale and Chita's contribution on Father McGiven's biography, who participated in the transformation of religious education in Zambia. They follow the changing contours of religious instruction and religion education in Zambia's political history through McGiven's personal experience of the subject.

Weisse's essay takes us out of the immediate school context, into the important role played by religious representatives in Hamburg. In pursuit of understanding the transformation of religious education at the University of Hamburg and its school projects, Weisse follows the transformative role played by religious leaders in the city. Returning us to the school, Kuusisto and Gearon focus on teachers in Finnish schools who share their views and life stories on the changing social and political context in which religion education is re-imagined.

With the next set of essays, we move out of the immediate contexts of schools. Mason takes us back to Africa to a slightly earlier period for a study of an inspiring teacher and educator. He examines the life and contribution of Francis Banks who, in a visionary way, challenged prevailing ideas of religious education in Grahamstown in the Eastern Cape in South Africa. Thurston's study on a Nigerian public intellectual shows how a public religious teacher navigates and shapes modernity and modernization. And last, but not least, Berglund's essay offers insight on a contemporary context through the life trajectory of a *hifz* (Qur'an memorization) teacher in the United Kingdom. She follows his journey from a deep immersion in a religious context to a more secular and inter-religious context.

The essays in this volume remind us that we need to pay more attention on the teachers, principals, managers and public intellectuals who shape and are shaped by the changing context of religion and religious education. The study of life trajectories shows that the lines between religion and religious education are blurred in personal life histories. They show that positions change through personal and contextual developments. And last, but not least, they point to the innovative and unexpected turns that individuals trace in their personal life journeys.

Acknowledgments

The articles presented in this special edition were presented at a conference in Cape Town in February 2016.

Notes

1. Patrick Crowly, "Paul Ricoeur: The Concept of Narrative Identity, the Trace of Autobiography," *Paragraph* 26, no. 3 (2003): 1–12; Paul Ricoeur, "Narrative Time," *Critical Inquiry* 7, no. 1 (1980): 169–190; Morny Joy (Ed.), *Paul Ricoeur and Narrative: Context and Contestation* (Calgary: University of Calgary Press, 1997).

2. Marjo Buitelaar and Hetty Zock (Eds.), *Religious Voices in Self-Narratives: Making Sense of Life in Times of Transition* (Berlin, Germany; Boston, MA: Walter de Gruyter, 2013).

3. Jill Lepore, "Historians Who Love Too Much: Reflections on Microhistory and Biography," *Journal of American History* 88, no. 1 (2001): 141.

4. Laura M. Carpenter, "Gendered Sexuality Over the Life Course: A Conceptual Framework," *Sociological Perspectives* 53, no. 2 (2010): 155–178; Caroline Laborde et al., "Trajectories and Landmark Events: How People Narrate Their Lives Analysis of Life Course Facts and Perceptions," *Population (English Edition)* (2007): 489–505; Marie Nathalie LeBlanc, "Versioning Womanhood and Muslimhood: 'Fashion' and the Life Course in Contemporary Bouaké, Côte D'Ivoire," *African: Journal of the International African Institute* 70, no. 3 (2000): 442–481; Miriam Rabelo and Iara Souza, "Temporality and Experience on the Meaning of Nervoso in the Trajectory of Urban Working-Class Women in Northeast Brazil," *Ethnography* 4, no. 3 (2003): 333–361.

5. Alexander Riley, "Crisis, Habitus, and Intellectual Trajectory," *Revue Européenne des Sciences Sociales* 42, no. 129 (2004): 307–314.

6. Peter I Costa, "From Refugee to Transformer: A Bourdieusian Take on a Hmong Learner's Trajectory," *TESOL Quarterly* 44, no. 3 (2010): 517–541.

RE Rooted in Principal's Biography

Ina ter Avest and Cok Bakker

ABSTRACT

Critical incidents in the biography of principals appear to be steering in their innovative way of constructing InterReligious Education in their schools. In this contribution, the authors present the biographical narratives of 4 principals: 1 principal introducing interreligious education in a Christian school, and 3 principals constructing a way of living apart together from a Christian, Islamic, and humanist point of view respectively. To understand (*Verstehen*) the principals' narratives and their innovative initiatiatives, the authors take as their theoretical frame of reference the concept of criticial incidents, the dialogical self theory, and the concept of materialized religion. From the analysis of the principals biographies, the authors arrive at a tentative conclusion that a solid education in a life orientation (be it humanistic, Christian, or Islamic) paired with an authentic curiosity toward "the other" seems to be preconditional for innovative actions in RE preparing pupils for a future they themselves are going to build.

It is the personality of the teacher that is of decisive importance in the way the formal curriculum is concretized in a lived curriculum in classes—in primary school as well as in secondary school and higher education. The personality of the teacher can be seen as the outcome of processes of family socialisation and professional socialisation in the context of the culture a teacher is raised and educated. It is not the teacher that is central in this article, but principals and their leadership in a team of teachers. In this article we explore the relation of the biography of the principal and the introduction of innovative ways of (inter-)religious education in his team, in the context of the plural society of the Netherlands.

In a changing society like the Netherlands, changing from homogeneity regarding people's religious worldview to a plurality of religious, secular, and so called multiple-belonging worldviews, principals of primary schools in different parts of the country explored innovative ways of religious education (RE) to adjust to this new situation. About 25 years ago in a small town in a rural area in the Netherlands, an inclusive way of interreligious education (IRE) was introduced in a Christian primary school, including Christian and Islamic RE classes, as well as classes of mutual recognition. About 10 years ago in the metropolitan area of Amsterdam, the Bijlmer district, principals of three primary schools with a different school ethos (public, Christian, and Islamic) decided to cooperate wherever possible and at the same time stick to their own school identity whenever necessary.

In the process of researching biographical narratives of principals, we tried to put together pieces of stories like in a jigsaw puzzle, attempting to interpret what was said in a way that does justice to their story, and to distinguish general themes and particular characteristics.

To structure the story of our research, we used an old Indian folk narrative ("The blind men and the elephant"), adapted for young children.[1] The adapted story is about different animals wondering about the identity of a newcomer in the wood. Each of the animals, the inhabitants of the wood, can perceive only a small part of the newcomer, guessing in a partial way the newcomer's identity. By bringing parts and pieces together at the end of the day they arrive at a shared conclusion. Similarly, by bringing together different complementary theoretical frameworks, and comparing different biographical narratives we will arrive at a preliminary conclusion regarding the future of religious/worldview education in difference.

The wood and its characteristics are presented in the first paragraph of this article; *the wood* representing the Dutch pillarized educational system. The theoretical framework is presented in the second paragraph. The core concept of Geert Kelchterman's theory on professional identity (critical incident) complemented with the core concepts of Hermans' valuation theory (VT) and the dialogical self theory (DST) and its self confrontation method (SCM, affective commitment), constitute the theoretical lenses through which we look at the principals' biographies. The third paragraph is dedicated to the principals' narratives—inhabitants of the wood—their life trajectory and the way they interpreted the newcomer, representing changes in the Dutch society. In the fourth paragraph the preliminary results of the analysis of the principals' narratives are presented and reflected upon, focusing on their relation with the materialization of religion in the subject of RE in their schools. Recommendations for future developments of RE in difference are formulated at the end of this contribution.

The wood: The Dutch pillarized system

In the Netherlands the educational system is characterized by so called pillars.[2] In each pillar a particular religious or secular world view dominates more or less the school's ethos and subsequently daily practices in the school.[3]

For a long time three types of schools constituted the pillarized system: Protestant schools, Roman-Catholic schools, and state schools. Two-and-a-half decade ago, a new type of schools was added to the Dutch educational system: the Islamic schools.[4] All schools in the Netherlands (including schools with a religious identity) are financially supported by the government, and controlled by the Inspectorate for Education.

The questions we try to answer in this contribution is: What critical incidents constitute a common thread in the personal and professional narrative of each of the pioneering principals (the make up of their professional identity),[5,6,7] What is the characteristic of this common thread, and how is this common thread concretized in their everyday practice of RE in their school?

Below we first present our theoretical framework, before we listen to the voices of the principal.

Theoretical framework

The focus of our research is on pioneering principals' critical incidents in their life trajectory, constituting the common thread in their narrative, and the possible relation with their initiative for some kind of teaching and learning in difference in the Dutch multicultural and multireligious society.[8]

Geert Kelchtermans

The concept of critical incident is central in Kelchterman's research and writings on teachers' subjective theory on education.[9] In interviews with teachers, Kelchtermans focuses on the verbal expressions about experiences in situations and, or with persons that apparently strongly influenced teachers' present day's subjective theory on education. Kelchtermans called these *critical incidents*. In his biographical interviews, Kelchtermans asks teachers to tell about their memories of their careers as a pupil and student. These experiences contribute to what Kelchtermans calls the "subjective educational theory" (cognitions about education). Together with the teacher's professional self-understanding (cognitions about one self as a teacher) this results in a personal interpretive framework for daily practices in the classroom, and subsequently daily actions and interactions with students.

Law focuses on the way people arrive at and handle these so called critical incidents[10] and distinguishes in this process the stages of sensing, sifting, focusing, and understanding what happened.[11] With the concept of sensing Law points to the aspect of gathering remarkable situations, without any information added yet about the meaning of such a situation. Sifting points to the search for causality by way of comparison between different remarkable situations. From this comparison of concrete situations abstract concepts and values emerge. In the next stages—focusing and understanding—through insights gained in the first two stages, a person arrives at the underlying story and value orientation of her or his professional carrere.

Hubert Hermans

Meijers and Lengelle follow Hermans and Hermans-Konopka in identifying professional identity as a dynamic multiplicity of personal (in contrast to social and cultural) positions or voices regarding work.[12] The concept of multi-voiced self, or dialogical self was introduced by Hermans and Kempen[13] and elaborated upon by Hermans and Hermans-Jansen.[14] Following these authors' line of thought we state that a variety of critical incidents are voiced in a so-called dialogical self constituting a plot in a person's narrative.[15] Interestingly, Hermans adds to Law's and Kelchtermans' cognitive approach to the affective commitment. Hermans fromulates it as a "valuation"—a one line description of a situation that evokes a mixture of feelings.

Birgit Meyer

Last but not least, Meyer in her public lecture at the Utrecht University focused on the material aspects of religion.[16] In her research Meyer studied the way people make religion happen in sets of practices, "in concrete acts that involve people, their body, things, pictures, texts and other media through which religion becomes tangibly present" and in what way religion plays a part in the development of a person's (religious or secular) worldview.[17] For Meijer the location of religion is in everyday's practice (the micro level of religious world-making), making the invisible visible and tangible. Religion, according to Meijer, refers to "particular, authorised and transmitted sets of practices ('sensational forms') and ideas aimed at 'going beyond the ordinary', 'surpassing' or 'transcending' or gesturing towards … 'the rest-of-what-is'."[18] This concept of materiality of religion, focusing on sensorial registers and multiple media (objects, rituals, texts, images) that can mediate between the immanent and the transcendents, paves the way for a clear sight on the particular way of concretization, materializing the common thread of principals' critical incidents in RE.

Inhabitants of the wood: Principals' life trajectory

Below we introduce four principals, innovators regarding RE in the Dutch multicultural and multireligious context. We had open interviews with these principals, asking them to reflect upon their life trajectory, according to the concept of wool gathering: gathering in retrospect important events in their upbringing and in their professional carreer. All four interviews were taperecorded and transcribed in verbatim, sent to the interviewees to correct misunderstandings or add information if needed for a better understanding. The analysis took place by way of sensing and sifting.

The first principal we introduce is the one who laid the foundations for interreligious education (see B., Principal of the Interreligious 'Juliana van Stolberg' Primary School). The three princiapals thereafter (see R., T., and C.) started the association of three schools with a different school ethos.

B., principal of the Interreligious 'Juliana van Stolberg' primary school

In his childhood, B. lived in the rural area in a village characterized by a conservative Christian climate, and so was the family of B. He remembers the teacher of Grade 6 telling stories in the church sevice of missionaries in New Guinea[19] resulting in B.'s wish to become a missionary. B. remembers that one evening the principal came to his father's house. B. himself was upstairs in his bedroom. "The house had wooden floors, I laid down, my ear against the floor and heard how—downstairs in the living—the principal begged my father to allow me to go to the gymnasium … Unfortunately my parents did not give permission to do so" because, according to them, "gymnasium is far too expensive, and besides that such an education is not for our kind of people." B.'s ambition was overruled by assumed values of "our kind of people.": "I feel sad when I remember this, at the same time also emotionally touched and grateful that this principal recognized my ambitions and pleaded for me." In that same period, B. recalls a text from the Bible read at his confirmation: "You shall be my witness." B. regarded this text as an inspiration for his innovative concretisation of interreligious education at the 'Juliana van Stolberg' primary school—"though in a different way than had the priest in mind at that moment, I think," B. adds smiling.

In 1973/1974, B. was principal of a Christian primary school in the southern part of the Netherlands. When the first Turkish children arrived in the classrooms of this school, the board of this Christian school became aware of the difference of these children. Board and teachers wondered, "Can we accept Muslim pupils in our Christian school?" According to B., this was a strange question, because the children with their origin in the islands of the Moluccas (one third of the school's population!) were Muslims as well. Until then, they had been approached and labeled as children from the former Dutch colony of Indonesia without any reflection on the religious identity of these families and their childeren. For B. this reflection process regarding a Christian school and Islamic children started when one of the Turkish pupils brought a booklet from home including stories about the prophet Isa (Jesus).

B.'s growing awareness and increasing interest to respond to religious and other differences moved quickly upon entering the 'Juliana van Stolberg' primary school, at that time a school with more than 200 pupils. A parallel experience was his awareness of the special educational needs of his physically handicapped son. This resulted in B.'s pedagogical approach to see the child not only in its needs for cognitive or physical development, but to include the background of the child, his upbringing in the family's value orientation, and "all that goes together with that" B. followed a course in Transcultural Pedagogics and Gestalt Psychology. Also he was supported by one of the board members to participate in a research project, 'Every Child Is a Child With Special Needs' a project on innovative experiments in education regarding children of minorities, as they were named in those days. "I recognised the 'special needs' of migrant children, the danger of being overruled by a school system." Parents favored Islamic RE during school hours, by an imam, because their children "hardly have any knowledge of Islam." The inclusion of the Islamic RE in a Christian school resulted in a proces of reflection on christian school identity and education by encounter. In 1989, The 'Juliana van Stolberg' primary school, until then under a board of Christian schools, continued its intercultural and interreligious approach.

A team of Christian and Islamic theologians from local religious communities in close cooperation with a psychologist and a musical teacher constructed a 3-year curriculum and developed lessons for interreligious RE classes: Christian classes and Islamic classes separately, and shared lessons—so-called 'lessons of recognition' a mix of teaching about and from religions. Narratives of religious traditions and from children's books, fairy tales, songs, and nursery rhymes as well as different kinds of practical activities materialized religion. These were used to invite the child in different ways to get to know its own tradition, to recognise the other's tradition and share what they have in common.[20]

How does this inhabitant of the wood, the Dutch pillarized society, perceive the newcomers? *Knowledge* and *recognition* of the other's otherness are keywords in this principal's biographical trajectory. "Knowing my roots, literally and metaphorically, are the make up of my identity." This principal's subjective religious education theory includes the man who saw him as an eager child with his educational needs, and his son's physical handicap that led him know the child-in-context and recognizing what the child brings into the school from the parents' house.

Principals of the association of three primary schools 'DE Brede School'

R., principal of the Islamic primary school 'As Soeffah'

R. was born in Surinam, a former Dutch colony in the northern part of South America. After more than 50 years living and working in the Netherlands, R. now lives in Surinam again, because "my roots are in Surinam."

R. is the youngest child in a family of nine childeren. During his childhood his father was imam in the main mosque in Surinam, his mother was a housewife. "In Surinam in a complete natural way people from different ethnic backgrounds, cultures and religions live together; living together in peace is grafted onto all in Surinam." Because R. was the youngest child, his father took him with him when he visited different religious communities. When R. was 17, he left his father's house and went to the Netherlands. R. was driven by curiosity and saw it as "an adventure to go to the Netherlands." Because there was a lack of money R. had to take a job during day time and followed courses during evening hours. He lived in lodgings that "I do not regret, but I missed my parents … there was no alternative, I made up my mind … it was a conscious choice!"

In the city of Groningen, R. was asked to be the imam of the Islamic community consisting of Muslims from all over the world. Part of the World Islamic Mission, related to the Sunni and Sufi streams of Islam, the Muslims in Groningen were brought together in one religious community in one mosque and were united in their prayers, despite their differences.

In the capital of Amsterdam, R. was asked to found an Islamic primary school. He became a member of the board and was appointed coordinator of founding and organising this Islamic school, inspired by the ideas of the World Islamic Mission. Motivated by his bridging experiences in Groningen, R. saw it "like an adventure, it was challenging to start a new school, not in the last place because of the resistance met by the boards of other schools in the neighbourhood." It was said that "an Islamic school can not meet the qualitative standards of good education." One day, one of the other schools instigated pupils to throw tomatoes at the trucks that carried the temporary units in which the Islamic school was supposed to be housed. "The muslim pupils were not allowed to play on its playground on Wednesday afternoons'" (when the children of this public school were at home!). On the question what moved R. to persevere, he answered, "I had made up my mind … it was a conscious choice, I had a mission!". R.'s mission was "to give each child what it needs, in particular to learn to live with differences, not only from a theoretical point of view, but even more so in practical situations. … Meeting each child's needs, that's my mission; stimulating the child's cognitive and social development and the conservation of her/his religious identity. "Regarding RE this means that for some children we had to start from scratch, since their parents did not practice Islam according to the rules." R. favors family learning in the sense that children bring home what they learn in school, thereby including the parents in their (religious) education.

The Islamic As Soeffah school started with 80 pupils. "Parents liked the way I concretised religious education, I sung songs, and I played games with the children." Parents were surprised; they were familiar with learning about the five pillars, about prayer, but "that it was possible to have fun learning Islam, for the parents was a surprising new aspect of their belief." Although a few parents objected in general against singing songs, they did not object against R. singing songs, because R. was part of their religious community, present at the mosque where he translated the sermons of the Urdu speaking Sufi imam. Characteristic for Sufi is "love for God, love for the prophet and love for the other." This love is materialized in RE in R's Islamic school in singing hymns and playing, and saying prayers five times a day, which reassured parents: "My child learns the right things in this school."

In cooperation with the public and secularized Christian school, R. states that a space is created for learning to live and work together: "There is no alternative, only by doing things together, people get to know and respect each other."

How does this inhabitant of the wood perceive the newcomers? *Curiousity* about the otherness of the other, together with the *awareness of urgency* to work and live together despite differences ("there is no alternative") are the main constituents of the thread of this principal's life trajectory. Added to this is R.'s willpower rooted in the critical incident in his adolescent life when he came to the Netherlands as a young boy of seventeen: "There was no alternative … I made up my mind … it was a conscious choice!"

T., principal of the public primary school 'Bijlmerhorst'

T. is raised in a Roman-Catholic family. He worked as a teacher at Curacao, a small island in the Caribian Sea, and former Dutch colony. One day an angry pupil shouted at him in the Papjamento language; this was not understood by T. When he asked a colleague about the meaning of what was said, this colleague explained it to him and added that he should "never accept a pupil shouting at him that way, this is a way slaves shout at their masters." This made T. aware of his whiteness amidst colored people, and of the history of which he is part, "whether I like it or not." In conflicts with teachers at work, he did not want people making it a colonial conflict, in the sense of "Now I have to bow my head, because the white master is speaking." Nor, the other way around, "What makes you speak like that? Are you aware of the pains your people caused in the lives of my forefathers?" For T. making jokes was, and still is, his way of living in difference, to endure what is different.

After a period in Curacao T. lived in the Antilles, a smaller group of islands in the Caribean, also a former Dutch colony. There he met his Antillian wife.

Over 400 pupils populated the primary school 'the Bijlmerhorst' when T. became the principal of this public primary school. With their poor and crowded families these pupils lived in appartment buildings that badly needed renovation. Another problem was the ethnic composition of his team: "Older Surinam women, not only born in Surinam, but also educated in Surinam, and subsequently adhering to a particular pedagogical approach." According to these teachers they did their work well when all the children were quiet "working and not asking questions, only saying something when the teacher asks them and not speaking up to the teacher." These two problems made it urgent for T. to look for partners to cooperate with. "I got to know R. the principal of the As Soeffah primary school and later also the principal C. of the Polsstok, with its buildings at the other side of the ring road." These three men liked each other, and that's how the cooperation started. In the autumn of 2001 "all of a sudden, out of the bleu, a million Euro's fell down from heaven! To be spent before the end of the year! ... This was a real stimulation to start to make serious plans for a shared educational vision and plan a new housing for our three schools. For T. financial reasons dominated, and "an identity based approach is lacking in the public school." "In general," T. states, "the description of a public school is a negative one: we are not christian, we are not supporting any belief system whatsoever."

According to T., a school identity is a solid framework for reflection, a verification of doing the right things. In T.'s opinion a lot could be learned by bringing the teams of the three schools together in a cooperative association. "In my school old Surinam teachers dominated pedagogical discussions. New perspectives would come in in a natural way, that's what I hoped from this cooperation." C. was inspiring at this stage "a real idealistic person, but I held back. I was not yet sure about R.'s position; would he be prepared to mix some water in the Islamic wine?"[21] T. had the impression that R. was more liberal, "or to put it in another way, more Surinam" than the other Islamic schools in Amsterdam. Next to that, T. thinks R. was the greater politician of the three principals. R.'s way of doing reminds T. of his experiences in Curacao and at the Antilles, where he learned that sometimes it's better not to explore and discuss differences in depth, but to take a distance and make a joke.

"I left 'the Bijlmerhorst' in 2003, I was tired. Working in the Bijlmerdistrict, in the Bijlmerhorst, drains your energy. ... The conflicts of every day practice are not just smaller differences of opinion. Underneath, however, there is this greater conflict of former slavery in the Dutch colony of Surinam." The way people respond to this kind of conflicts is imbued with unexpressed feelings of supremacy paired with guilt, T. states.[22] "There are not many white, Dutch people who force others to adapt to our way of living, however, there are many ways in which implicitly these people exclude others."

In the school where T. works these days, narratives from different traditions are included in RE, "narratives about others to learn about your self." T. and his team aim at creating moments of encounter—meetings with different people in real life as well as in "narratives, different people with different value orientations, solving conflicts, thinking about existential questions, and living their everyday life in difference."

How does this inhabitant of the wood, the Dutch pillarized society, perceive the newcomers? *Inclusion* of the other's uniqueness and a continuous exploration of ways to endure differences are important ingredients of the common thread of T.'s narrative, rooted in the critical incidents with his team consisting of mainly poor educated Surinam teachers. According to T. every school and every teacher has to explore his or her positionality regarding differences in its relation to the construction of RE or secular worldview education in the particular situation of *this* school and *these* pupils. "It is an everlasting search for good RE and at the same time a search for points of reference for good RE."

C., principal of the secularized Christian primary school 'Polsstok'

C. was born deaf in a conservative Roman Catholic family. At the age of 4, as a result of an accident, the ability to hear was regained. From early childhood, C. has "learned to face situations and discover possibilities and chances." C. states that he moves "towards the Light, God; that's what moves and motivates me." His mother taught him to be "the good Samaritan"; his father was more straight forward and favored learning by doing, which resulted in "becaming aware of what I did not want, and taking the freedom to make my own choices."

In his family the border line between good and bad behavior was very clear. In adolescence he learned that it is not as simple as that. "What I missed in my youth is the recognition that there are different value systems, that are good in their own way." Some values C. took with him throughout his life, like equality of all people, respect for the other, integrety. A saying that has influenced his life is, "When people are hungry, don't give the fish, but teach them to catch a fish." In his teams in complex situations this has resulted in the question "is it about eating or fishing?"

C. worked in Indonesia as a language teacher for a couple of years. "I jumped into a situation in which I knew nothing, and was forced to ask questions." He allowed his pupils now and then to sit on his chair and give tasks to their classmates. Master and pupils changed roles; by doing so C. learned a lot about the child's perspective.

Transactional Analysis and Neuro Linguistic Programming are but two of the courses C. participated in to enrich and structure his knowledge and experiences. "I like to explore new ways; I always see new possibilites, chances."

In 2007, a serious eye injury was diagnosed. He lost over 50% of his sight, which according to his board in those days made it impossible for C. to be a class teacher anymore. Looking for other possibilities C. applied for a position as principal of a primary school, which was agreed upon by his board.

C. favors teaching and learning, keeping in mind the product with a focus on the process. In the process the teacher is at times professional educator, coach, and friend according to the developmental needs of the child. "It's important to be able and to take responsability to switch roles when it's needed."

Encounter is a keyword in C.'s subjective education theory. "Go and visit each other in the classroom, ask questions, and see what you can learn from each other." The same holds for children: wonder about "the other's otherness, ask questions and enrich your point of view." When a parent comes to C.'s office, complaining, C. tells himself not to forget about the reciprocal aspect of any communication. We both, the sender and the receiver, should take a we-perspective. If both "I's are prepared, willing and able to take the 'we'-perspective a dialogue can start." According to C. it's important to give arguments for decisions, to give words to inner motivations, to express feelings. "We hardly do that in education. Teachers should be a role model in telling their pupils what they do and why."

In a similar way, according to C., the tension is felt between the autonomy of the parent and the school's perspective. "The moment I judge a parents' way of doing as wrong, I cannot see the different shades of 'good' anymore." C. is of the opinion that staying in touch with the other, also in situations of conflicting interests, is very important. "Such conversations are not always pleasant, though very valuable because of establishing clear boundaries." As such, according to C., in these conversations teachers and parents are role models for the children, "already a child of four has to learn to on the one hand to mark border lines and on the other hands to be prepared to cross boundaries."

"Pillarization is out, cooperation is in," according to C. "We have to learn to live amidst different value orientations and respond to that in a proper way." This also holds for different religious orientations. "Learning from and with each other" is the core of religious education in C.'s school and as such part of citizenship education. Creating spaces for encounter C. sees as core business in education, "a space to learn from each other's value orientations, provides some straws in the wind in times of transition." "*Vreedzame school* (Education for Peace)[23] in that sense is a promising concept to elaborate upon," according to C.

C. favors the development of a "pedagogical constitution" for the three schools-in-context, structuring a space for encounter, awareness of the other's and one's own choices based on different religious or secular world views.

How does this principal interpret the development from a homogenous to a diverse Dutch society; how does he perceive the newcomers? Perceiving *chances* in the encounter with the other-who-is-different, asking *questions* about unfamiliar and different ways of behavior and *change of perspective*, together constitute the common thread in this principal's approach of the other, be it a pupil, a teacher or a parent/caretaker. According to C. we should open our eyes and hearts for "possibilities, instead of focusing on impossibilities"—this clearly is related to his criticial incident of losing sight. C. is of the opinion that the encounter with the other, staying in touch with the other, however different the other may be, is of utmost importance.

"The plural of togetherness is future"

R. situates the start of the association of the three schools in the Amsterdam project Heart and Soul, in which the As Soeffah school participated with its pupils. Children were the guides for children from other religious communities visiting the mosque; a child-to-child introduction—an innovative way of encounter initiated by R.

In this cooperation, principals (and not the boards!) took the lead and took the responsibility. R. convinced his board and the parents, warning them for the intensification of the controversy in the Dutch society. "Cooperating with the other schools means they will speak up for us" – which T[24]. in particular really did, R. adds. R. took away parents' fear. "If your child meets a Christian child, then s/he will become more aware of the own Islamic religiosity. ... In the encounter your child will learn the practice of respect. Surely, we all wish our children to live in peace!"

Reflecting upon the start of the process of cooperation and in particular planning the housing for the three schools, T. thinks that, "a great mistake was that the principals were the active stimulators, whereas the boards had not really committed themselves to this whole process—in particular regarding the financial consequences of this cooperation. An indepth discussion with the boards might have resulted in a serious conflict," and we did not want to spend time to conflict resolution, we wished to go on with the construction of the building for housing of the three schools, as well as in a more idealistic sense in bringing teams with different (religious and secular) world views and educational views together to learn with and from each other."

According to C. it was

> ... in my interest to have a solid public and Islamic partner. ... First of all we explored what we have in common, resulting in celebrating Christmas together. Later we were able to face the differences, for example the differences in rituals regarding existential experiences, like the death of a beloved person.... Each of us brings with him his own ideals from his own life trajectory, which is a constituting element for a shared future. ... It's more interesting to explore differences, because they are the start for interesting and instructive conversations.

C. is of the opinion that "you cannot watch over your own courtyard without being in touch with your neighbours."

The three principals agreed upon the slogan of the association of their schools named 'DE Brede School'[25] in the Bijlmer district: "The plural of togetherness is future."[26]

Conclusions: Completing the jigsaw puzzle?

Now that we are informed about the different critical incidents and the thread in the narrative of each of the inhabitants of the wood, we take a closer look at similarities and differences.

Similarities and differences in biographies

First of all we see some similarities in these principals' biographies: they are all men and members of the same generation—a generation that was raised in a period of peace, increasing economic prosperity, and subsequently an increase of possibilities for education and training. This so called "baby boom" or "protest"-generation is characterized by their idealistic view on society and their search for social cohesion—aspects that are clearly present in the four biographies. However, also a characteristic of the so called Generation X is clearly present: all four of them respond to society's growing diversity in a constructive way.[27] All four of them have a degree in teacher training, two of them continued their education in in-service trainings, a characteristic of life long learning of the Generation X.

All four principals enjoyed a solid and articulated socialization in a religious tradition—both in the family, in school and at the Teacher Training Institute. Each of them became aware of the historical context they live and work in, partly due to the fact that they—literally—crossed boundaries and had to respond to the confrontation with another culture—including religion—by living abroad for a while. Their narratives inform us of a mixture of emotions in the way they value their disruptive moments that—at the end of the day—taught them to encourage others, their teachers, pupils and parents, to open up for the other, which is only possible if and only if "we ourselves are willing to pass the revolving door of our own truth."[28] Not overwhelmed by their emotions in a responsibility by conviction, but informed by a responsibility by ethics each of them has been and still is motivated in his actions in responding to the challenges of living in diversity.[29]

We see some striking differences in these principals' biographies. Principal R. was raised as a Muslim in Surinam, whereas the others were raised in Christian families in the Netherlands.

"Going abroad" for R. was going to the Netherlands; for the others it meant going to another country than the Netherlands. Principal T. stayed in the Netherlands because Curacao and the Antilles in those days were part of the kingdom of the Netherlands, and Principal C. lived in Indonesia—a former Dutch colony—where he gave Dutch language lessons. The focus of the principals emerging from their life trajectory are slightly different.

B. focuses knowing the child-in-context and responding to every child as a child with special needs. This resulted in a model for RE that recognizes the religious background of the child (Christian or Islamic), at the same time broadening the pupils' horizon by organizing moments of encounter in RE classes during school hours.

R.'s focus is on curiosity and urgency, "there is no alternative," to work together in spite of many differences in the Islamic religious community. Although he left his father's house in Surinam in his teens, he was steadfast regarding his father's open attitude to different faiths. It is this attitude of openness that is concretized in RE in the Islamic school—openness towards different schools of Islam the parents adhere to, and openness towards other partners in the association of schools.

T. stresses the inclusion of the other's uniqueness and a continuous exploration of ways to endure differences, resulting in a focus on contextuality of education: it's all about this school and these pupils. Regarding RE, or as he named it, worldview education or citizenship education, he introduced story telling, inviting teachers to tell stories from different cultural and religious traditions, including fairy tales and folk stories.

In his subjective educational theory, C.'s focus is on the capability of perceiving chances in the encounter with the other-who-is-different, asking questions about unfamiliar ways of behavior, and change of perspective. Teachers are trained by a Christian coach to teach their pupils and develop their competences in changing perspective and as a result these classes have a Christian flavor combined with an open attitude towards other beliefs.

Recognition of the other, the child-in-context shows to be the common thread in the narratives of these four pioneering principals. Firstly, because "there is no alternative" to openness and cooperation. Secondly, there is an unconditioned curiosity for the other. All four principals share the need to know one's tradition, and to develop an open attitude towards the other's tradition.[30]

With lenses consisting of the main concept of Kelchterman's theory we see a relation of their subjective education theory with critical incidents. The child B. lying on the floor and listening to the principal's plea for the gymnasium is such a critical incident. In R.'s story, his journey to the Netherlands at the age of seventeen is a critical incident, as is the situation where children hindered the delivery of temporary housing for the As Soeffah primary school. T.'s critical incidents inform us about misunderstanding, because of differences in interpretations, related to the colonial past of the Netherlands. T. has developed a way of denying what you feel, although he is more in favour of expressing his feelings in a straight orward way. C's critical incident has to do with his physical handicaps: being born deaf and losing almost all of his sight in his forties. These critical incidents are interwoven for the respective principals in their common thread as described above.

We see a decisive role for a mixture of affective relations, as they come to the fore in each of the narratives. As an affect-loaden valuation, B.states, "I lay down, my ear against the wooden floor, as a sponge sucking the words of my principal pleading for me to go to the gymnasium." In a similar way we hear positive and negative emotions when R. describes in his life trajectory the Surinam situation with different religions and traditions. Regarding his feelings T. talks about the mixed feelings he has in his professional relationship with his Surinam colleagues. Emotions are clear in the statement of C. when he refers to his loosing his sight and being forced to change his perspective from loss and subsequent *im*possibilities, to chances and their possibilities.

The lenses of Meijer's concept of materialized religion open our eyes for "the outward manifestations" and "concrete acts that involve people", that are present in the interreligious school of B., in the Islamic school of R. and in the open christian school of C. In RE classses these concrete acts, and the meaning thereof for classmates and their parents are related to a religious tradition. Everyday practice of religion, according to Meijer the microlevel of religious world-making, in the three associated schools in the Bijlmer district is stimulated by the introduction of *Vreedzame School* (Education for Peace).

Each of the principals admits a strong commitment to the heritage of materialized religious traditions. Their respective heritage imbues their efforts in the innovative processes regarding RE in their school. Religious tradition has been a source for understanding their own life. Suprisingly similar are the principal's ideas regarding how religions should be materialized in the future: in dialogue with the narrative of the other, be it in real life—at a grass roots level—or in narratives; there is no alternative! RE and worldview education in this way is located in a praxis of "provocative pedagogy."[31] This pedagogy challenges teachers, pupils and their parents, and caring for them at the same time, bound together as fellow citizens of the Dutch plural society.

More research is needed on the mutual interpretation of theories and theoretical concepts. Such a mutual interpretation is like the disturbing perception and by consequence its reception of the familiar drawing of 'My wife and my mother in law' (drawn by the cartoonist W.E. Hill, published for the first time in *Puck Magazine* in 1915). The ugly nose of the mother in law/a nasty witch at the same time is the well-shaped cheek of the wife/a beautiful young women; the black hair articulating the ugliness of the witch at the same time accentuates the beauty of the young lady. In a similar way such a disturbing perception and reception of theoretical concepts will open up for new perspectives and subsequent creative interpretations.[32]

From theoretical research amongst others by Van den Ende and Kunneman (2008),[33] and practical research by Bakker and Rigg (2004)[34] and Day et al.[35] we know already quit a bit about the teachers's life trajectory in relation to her/his way of teaching in her/his classes, little is known sofar about principal's critical incidents and the relation with their way of implementing innovative practices and models of IRE in her/his school. We recommend more research on principals' life trajectories and the way IRE mirrors the process of wool gathering in their biographies.

We recommend more research to reflect upon the way these kinds of IRE and worldview education in primary schools can be integrated in (religion/worldview related) citizenship education in the Netherlands. In what way can all pupils in all Dutch schools—independent of their religious or secular school identity—be taught and learn about, with and from each other, integrating knowledge about different religious and secular worldviews into an attitude of openness and curiosity—preconditional for dialogue.

Last but not least we recommend longitudinal research to increase our body of knowledge about the effects of the above described practices and models of IRE on the life trajectory of children and young adolescents who attended these classes, and their integration and active participation in Dutch society. They surely are the citizens who build the Dutch plural society, being work-in-progress.

Notes

1. M. Rinck, *Ik Voel Een Voet* [I Sense A Foot] (Rotterdam, The Netherlands: Lemniscaat).
2. I. ter Avest, C. Bakker, G. D. Bertram-Troost, and S. Miedema, "Religion and Education in the Dutch Pillarized and Post-Pillarized Educational System: Historical Backgrounds and Current Debates," in *Religion and Education in Europe. Developments, Contexts and Debates*, ed. R. Jackson, S. Miedema, W. Weisse, and J.-P. Willaime (Münster, Germany: Waxmann, 2007), 203ff.
3. G. D. Bertram-Troost, S. Miedema, C. Kom, and I. ter Avest, "A Catalogue of Dutch Primary Schools in the Secular Age: Empirical Results," *Religion & Education* 42, no. 2 (2015): 202–17.
4. B. Budak, C. Bakker, and I. ter Avest. "Identity development in the first two Islamic schools in the Netherlands," in *European Perspectives on Islamic Education and Public Schooling*, edited by J. Berglund (Sheffield, UK: Equinox, 2017).
5. T. van den Ende and H. Kunneman, "Normatieve Professionaliteit en Normatieve Professionalisering," in *Goed werk. Verkenning van Normatieve Professionaliteit*, ed. G. Jacobs, R. Meij, H. Tenwolde, and J. Zomer (Amsterdam, The Netherlands: SWP, 2008), 68–87.
6. C. Bakker and E. Rigg, *De Persoon van de Leerkracht; Tussen Schoolidentiteit en Leerlingendiversiteit* (Zoetermeer, The Netherlands: Meinema, 2004).
7. C. Bakker, *Het Goede Leren. Leraarschap als Normatieve Professie* (Utrecht, The Netherlands: Hogeschool Utrecht, 2014).
8. B. Roeben, *Godsdienstpedagogiek van de hoop* [Pedagogy of RE of Hope] (Leuven/Voorburg, The Netherlands: Acco, 2007).
9. G. Kelchtermans, *De Professionele Ontwikkeling van Leerkrachten in Het Basisonderwijs Vanuit Het Biografisch Perspectief* [The professional development of teachers in primary education from a biographic perspective] (Leuven, The Netherlands: Universitaire Pers Leuven, 1994). See also G. Kelchtermans, "Who I Am in How I Teach is the Message: Self-understanding, Vulnerability and Reflection," *Teachers and Teaching: Theory and Practice* 15, no. 2 (2009): 257–72.
10. *Critical incidents* have different names: "boundary experiences" (Meijers and Lengelle 2012); "disruptive moments (ter Avest 2014); "turning points" (Kuusisto 2016), to name just a few.
11. F. Meijers, and R. Lengelle, "Narratives at Work: The Development of Career Identity", *British Journal of Guidance & Counselling* 40, no. 2 (2012): 157–176. doi:10.1080/03069885.2012.665159.
12. Ibid.
13. H. Hermans and H. Kempen, *The Dialogical Self: Meaning as Movement* (San Diego, CA: Academic Press, 1993).
14. H. J. M. Hermans and E. Jansen, *Self-Narratives: The Construction of Meaning in Psychotherapy* (New York, NY: The Guilford Press, 1995).
15. Ibid., see also H. J. M. Hermans and A. Hermans-Konopka, *Dialogial Self Theory. Positioning and Counter-Positioning in a Globalizing Society* (Cambridge, MA: Cambridge University Press, 2010).
16. B. Meyer, *Mediation and the Genesis of Presence. Towards a Material Approach to Religion*, Public Lecture (Amsterdam, The Netherlands: Utrecht University, 2012).

17. Ibid., 7.
18. Ibid., 23.
19. A former Dutch colony, nowadays part of the Republic of Indonesia.
20. I. ter Avest, "Dutch Children and Their God", *British Journal of Religious Education* 31, no. 3 (2009): 251–62. doi:10.1080/01416200903112425
21. The Dutch saying is "to add some water to the wine, which means: changing your point of view, in the sense of toning down, widening the scope.
22. See also: G. Wekker, *White Innocence: Paradoxes of Colonialism and Race* (Durham, NC: Duke University Press, 2016).
23. 'Vreedzame School' (Education for Peace) is the name of the teaching materials used in the three schools involved in the association of the three schools.
24. T. is the principal of the public school involved.
25. 'DE Brede School'—inclusive education in DE neighbourhood of the Bijlmer district; DE referring to the names of the street in this neighbourhood that all start deliberately with the capital D or E.
26. In Dutch, "Het meervoud van samen is toekomst."
27. A. C. Bontekoning, "Generaties in Organisaties [Generations in organisations]" (Doctoral thesis, Tilburg University, Tilburg, the Netherlands, 2007).
28. P. Scheffer, *De Vrijheid van de Grens* [The freedom of the boundary]. Stichting Maand van de Filosofie (2016), 19.
29. Ibid., 59.
30. R. Burggreave, *From Self-Development to Solidartiy. An ethical Reading of Human Desire in tis Socio-Political Relevance according to Emmanuel Levinas* (Leuven, The Netherlands: Peeters, Center for Metaphysics and Philosophy of God, Institute of Philosophy, 1985).
31. I. ter Avest and G. D. Bertram-Troost (eds.), *Geloven in samen leven* [Faith in living together] (Amsterdam, the Netherlands: Science Guide, 2009).
32. See A. Visser in his farewell lecture *Theorieën vanbinnen en vanbuiten* [Theories from an inside and outside perspective] (The Netherlands, Utrecht University, April 22, 2016). http://www.uu.nl/agenda/afscheid-van-albert-visser-meld-u-nu-aan
33. T. van den Ende and H. Kunneman, "Normatieve Professionaliteit en Normatieve Professionalisering," in *Goed werk. Verkenning van Normatieve Professionaliteit*, ed. G. Jacobs, R. Meij, H. Tenwolde, and J. Zomer (Amsterdam, the Netherlands: SWP, 2008), 68–87.
34. C. Bakker and E. Rigg, *De Persoon van de Leerkracht; Tussen Schoolidentiteit en Leerlingendiversiteit* (Zoetermeer, the Netherlands: Meinema, 2004).
35. D. V. Day, P. Gronn, and E. Salas, "Leadership Capacity in Teams," *The Leadership Quaterly* 15 (2004): 857–880. (Cited in: A. Hargreaves and M. Fullan. *Professional capital: Transforming teaching in every school* (New York, NY: Teachers College Press, 2012).)

Trailing a Missionary Teacher's Position and Contributions in Zambian Religious Education

Nelly Mwale and Joseph Chita

ABSTRACT

This article focuses on the biography of a missionary teacher (Thomas McGivern) who has contributed to the development of Zambian religious education (RE). It uses a qualitative case study design to capture and understand the unique position and contributions of the missionary and teacher to Zambian RE. The article argues that McGivern's aspirations have been embraced in the RE syllabus to date. The missionary teacher's involvement in RE also mirrors the changing dynamics that shaped the subject from religious instruction to RE.

Zambian Religious Education (RE) owes its development to efforts of Christian missionaries such as Fr. Thomas McGivern. Despite the literature acknowledging the role of the missionaries in the development of RE as a curriculum subject, little attention has been paid to individual contributions and the principles held, which shaped and influenced the subject. Therefore, without historicizing the growth of Zambian RE, the scope of this article is limited to the account of a missionary teacher (Thomas McGivern) who has contributed to RE over time and is seen by many as the father of Zambian RE.[1] The article acknowledges that numerous individuals have made tremendous contributions to Zambian RE as it is today, but only focuses on Thomas McGivern as a way of celebrating his career. This is especially pertinent as he was attacked and wounded by thieves in 2011 and lost his memory. Paying homage to his memory from his favorite quote: "A person is alive as long as he is remembered and dead only by forgetfulness,"[2] this article will keep him alive as it reflects on his contributions and his inspiration. As Tayob[3] remarks, biographies tell a great deal about people in a particular context.

Here too, the life trajectory of the missionary teacher mirrors the changes that RE has undergone in the Zambian context over time.

Studies on RE in Zambia have examined the growth and development of RE.[4] The role of missionaries in the curriculum development of RE in Zambia has also been explored.[5] In addition, Mujdrica[6] has evaluated the three Zambian secondary school RE syllabuses (junior, 2044 and 2046), whereas Simuchimba[7] investigated RE in Zambia with reference to the syllabuses, approaches, and contentious issues. The studies show that the aims of RE have changed from a focus on converting pupils and nurturing them in the Christian faith to helping them to learn about religions in a critical manner.[8] The aims of current RE also seek to help learners to develop the ability to make reasoned and informed judgments about religious and moral issues with reference to the teaching of all religious traditions in Zambia. The change does not examine the individual contributions of different personalities who have been behind these developments. We argue that following some personalities would help us understand the form current Zambian RE has taken and its future.

The reflection on McGivern as a missionary teacher is deemed significant for the understanding of current Zambian RE. We also hope to contribute to scholarship on Zambian RE, which has largely been centered on its general history. The article is also deemed important in filling the gap of a lack of documentation on some of the notable personalities in Zambian RE. A missionary teacher is taken to mean an individual who other than having a Christian commission to come to Zambia and spread the gospel[9] was involved in teaching, perfecting, administration, and management of the Zambian formal schooling system.

Context

Zambia became an independent nation from Britain in 1964, embraced multi-party democracy up to 1972 when it changed to a one-party system of governance.[10] The latter lasted up to until 1991 when the country reverted to a multi-party system of democratic governance.[11] In terms of religious demographics, McGivern worked in a context where Christianity was and is the dominant religion in Zambia, though not undermining the existence of Zambian traditional religion (incorporated in Zambian culture). The country was also declared a Christian nation in 1991.

Until the early 21st century, Zambia's Christianity was referred to in terms of three mother bodies, also known as umbrella bodies: the Zambia Episcopal Conference (ZEC) now the Zambia Conference for Catholic Bishops, the Council of Churches in Zambia (CCZ), and the Evangelical Fellowship of Zambia (EFZ).[12] The CCZ was established in 1945 as the umbrella body of mainline Protestant churches. Officially instituted in 1963, the ZEC is the administrative body of all Roman Catholic dioceses. It was this administrative body that McGivern had to report to, represent, and work with. The Evangelical Fellowship of Zambia was officially formed in 1964 to oversee evangelical churches. In 2001 a fourth umbrella body, the Independent Churches Organization of Zambia (ICOZ), was formed to bring together charismatic churches, ministries, fellowships, and centers.

Cheyeka reported that of Zambia's population (14,222,000), 95.5% were Christians, 0.5% was Muslims, 0.1% was Hindus, whereas other and non-affiliated categories accounted for 2% and 1.9%, respectively.[12] All these religious traditions have not replaced indigenous religions, as was the case in other southern African countries.[13]

The education system in Zambia consists of 7 years of primary and 5 years of secondary schooling before pupils can enter college, university, or other institutions of higher learning.[14] The first 7 years of education are compulsory, from age 7 to 14 years. Transition from lower to higher educational levels is determined by the performance of the pupils in national examinations at the end of 12 years.[15]

Since independence, the education system has witnessed a number of policies promulgated to guide education. These include the 1977 educational reforms whose focus was on the development of the whole person,[16] the 1992 Focus on Learning, the 1996 Educating Our Future, and the current 2013 Zambia Education Curriculum framework. In 2013, the Government developed a new school curriculum that would enable learners to choose a career path.[17] According to the Ministry of Education, the move is expected to accord learners an opportunity to academically progress in line with their abilities and interests.[18]

The new education framework mainly focuses on incorporating current areas of social, economic, and technological developments in the curriculum and the opening of two career pathways at secondary school level (academic and vocational). Others include the linking of school vocational curriculum to technical and vocational training programs, and integration of some subjects with interrelated and similar competences and content into learning areas. The new curriculum also spells out key competences to be achieved by learners at every level of education.

As a curriculum subject, RE is taught at different levels. At primary, it is taught as part of the integrated social sciences, while at secondary it has remained as an independent optional subject. There are two RE syllabuses, the first called 2044 and commonly taught in grant-aided schools, and the second, 2046, taught in public schools. Most importantly, it should be noted that unlike other countries like Britain and South Africa, Zambia lacks a national policy on RE, which ideally should emanate from the country's constitutional provisions on religion and education, and shape the preferred model of RE that the country can adopt.

Conceptualization of religious education and related terms

The varying usage of the concept RE can be problematic if left unattended to, thus ideas from other scholars offer insights into the usage of the concepts.

Halstead[19] described RE as education in religion, or as education about religion. The former is synonymous with religious instruction (RI), the type designed to nurture young people in a particular faith, also meant to preserve faith in a particular religious group and across generations. RI can be presented either formally or informally, formally when it occurs at home, places of worship, or in public schools where the majority citizens share one religious faith, and denominational schools (private or state-funded). Sometimes RI is identical to catechesis, whose aim is faith development through transmission of religious teachings. RE as RI has been identified with some weaknesses, such as neglect of liberal values associated with critical openness and personal autonomy among others, the manner of presentation in which it is taught as truth beliefs, its definition of knowledge as dogma, revelation instead of rationally justified beliefs, and failure to prepare children for life in a multi-faith-cultural society.[19]

RE as education about religion aims to develop knowledge and understanding of religion, where learners are free to develop their own faith. Through this type of RE, learners come to learn about other religions but are not expected to develop personal commitment. The aim of such an RE is to produce religious literacy. This type of RE has been critiqued for reducing revealed truth to cultural practices and undermining commitment to any faith.

Jackson also acknowledged a third system in which the first two types are mixed. He gave an example of England and Wales "where fully funded schools have a form of religious education which aims at impartiality in its treatment of religion, while mainly state-funded voluntary aided schools may teach and promote the religion of the sponsoring body."[20] Jackson and Hull added that the three types can best be distinguished through the aim of the subject, that is: Educating into, about, and from religion:[21]

> Educating into religion deals with a single religious tradition, taught by "insiders" and often has the objective of enabling pupils to come to believe in the religion or to strengthen their commitment to it. Educating about religion confines itself to using descriptive and historical methods, and aims neither to foster nor to erode religious belief. Educating from religion involves pupils in considering different responses to religious and moral issues, so that they may develop their own views in a reflective way.

The history of RE in Zambia to some extent has similar characteristics as the three types of RE offered by Halstead, Jackson, and Hull. In fact, it is a mishmash that shows overlap of one type into the other. This article therefore shows the attempt to move from RI to RE in McGivern's career.

Methodological approach

The article used a descriptive case study design. Creswell[22] noted that case study research is a qualitative approach in which the investigator explores a bounded system (a case) or multiple bounded systems (cases) over time, through detailed, in-depth data collection involving multiple sources of information (including observations, interviews, audiovisual material, and documents and reports). A descriptive case study was used because the article sought to provide a narrative account of the contributions of a missionary teacher. This was also because the article focused on an individual actor (missionary teacher) to understand his perception of events.[23]

The article used document review, archival records, and interviews as methods of data collection to maximize the strengths and minimize the weaknesses of the methods used.[24] The personal interviews took 30–45 minutes and respondents were encouraged to feel free to share their experiences, which they reflected upon after the interviews, and the response was overwhelming too. The interview questions were centered on exploring the career of the missionary teacher in RE, the positions and contributions made to RE and why such contributions were made. Other individuals such as lecturers (two) of RE at the University of Zambia, and others who lived with missionaries and with McGivern in particular were also interviewed. In total, seven respondents participated in the study (three missionary teachers who lived and worked with McGivern, two university lecturers who worked with McGivern, one missionary who lived with McGivern, and a former member of the Zambia Association for Religious Education Teachers founded by McGivern). The data was thematically analyzed.

We note that there are other teachers or personalities who could and have contributed to Zambian RE, but the life story of McGivern serves to reflect the changing positions and perceptions of the subject and how his position shaped his contributions to RE. McGivern's biography mirrors the developments that RE has under gone over time in the Zambian context. This is also because the story of Zambian RE is one that has failed from an ecumenical perspective, as the catholic and protestant divisions are still alive in this self-proclaimed Christian nation. The article argues that by reflecting on McGivern's biography, lessons can be drawn for developing a relevant RE in twenty-first century Zambia. The findings from this study may therefore not be generalized, but instead they can be used as stepping-stones toward an understanding of contributions, which have been made to Zambian RE in the different stages of its development.

Brief perspectives on the growth and development of Zambian RE

As has been documented, the growth and development of RE in the Zambian education system is attributed to early missionary education in which RI was at the center of the school system. Simuchimba[25] notes that in this missionary era, the subject was used to emphasize the doctrines and beliefs of particular denominations. It was during this period that McGivern and other Jesuit Scholastics were sent on a mission to Northern Rhodesia. Like others, he fostered education into religion, when he taught in the third grade at Chikuni Mission.

When government took over the responsibility for education, religion had to justify its inclusion in the school timetable. The process of developing from RI to RE began in 1970 with a meeting of religion tutors at eight primary teachers colleges (four of these were church-run colleges and four-government run) to discuss their problems and future. They quickly realized that a common syllabus and textbooks for the whole country would be of great benefit. Within a year, they produced a syllabus and an example of one textbook. Both the Christian Council and Catholic Episcopal Conference supported the venture, and the Ministry of Education was delighted with such a show of unity. By 1972, all stakeholders approved the agreed syllabus for RE, and the textbooks followed.

A year later, the East African "Developing in Christ" series for junior secondary classes was approved for all schools. The introduction of the two agreed syllabuses was educationally significant in that from that time RI or scripture, as the subject was sometimes referred to in official documents, "began to be called 'Religious Education' and so 'began to take its place in the educational policy of Zambian schools.'"[26]

In 1973, Zambia adopted the Socialist One Party socioeconomic and political system which had its own impact on the development of RE. To start with, the Ministry of Education's *Education for Development* draft proposal was formulated to provoke national debate and steer the country's education system in the socialist direction. However, there was no specific mention of RE throughout the relevant chapter on curriculum, a situation, which threatened the churches and other stakeholders. Therefore, after a thorough debate, the concerns raised by the churches were addressed in the 1977 policy document, *Educational Reform: Proposals and Recommendations* whose aim was to create a system of education, which is properly attuned to, and more fully meets the needs and aspirations of Zambians.[27] RE was included in the curriculum under a new name or area of learning called "Spiritual and Moral Education."[28] RE became somewhat more Zambian and pluralistic. This gave rise to new syllabuses that were introduced at the secondary level and these were 2044 and 2046, a Zambianized version of Christian Living Today and Cambridge Bible Knowledge, respectively.[29]

For the first time, non-Christian religions such as Hinduism, Islam, and Indigenous Zambian Religions were included in the syllabus, as well as humanist and socialist values to respond to the pluralist and multi-faith Zambian society.[30] Therefore, the new RE syllabuses, which incorporated the 1977 Education policy document, were introduced in 1982 and 1984/ 1986 for junior and senior secondary, respectively. The syllabuses were also a response to State attempts to bring humanist socialist ideas and influence in all areas of national life including education. More so, the education policy was that of massive expansion, elaboration, and Africanization of existing colonial structures.[31]

The paradox of having Christian syllabuses that incorporated other religions is clearly exemplified in the aim of the subject which was:

> To enable pupils to appreciate spiritual, moral and religious values and behavior … The appreciation is drawn from the four main religious traditions in Zambia (namely, Christianity, Hinduism, Indigenous Zambian beliefs and Islam) and from the religious elements of the Zambian philosophy of Humanism.[32]

This shows that though the names or titles of the syllabuses and content (2046 included 82% Christian material, whereas 2044 had 56%) had remained overly Christian, a shift toward embracing other religious traditions was also evident.

In 1991, a new political regime (Movement for Multi Party Democracy) was ushered into power. This also marked a new era for RE from a policy perspective. For example, after the 1977 education reforms, the 1990s were characterized by two major policy documents (*Focus on Learning* of 1992 and *Educating Our Future* of 1996). *Focus on learning* replaced the Education Reform document, which had been in force since 1977. With regard to RE, the subject fell more under state control than before. In response to *Focus on Learning*'s critique, a National Symposium to review the school curriculum was held in August 1993 and the RE subject Panel or Review Team was an eight-member panel, which included the Inspector of Religious Education (Fr. T. McGivern).

The team revised the 1982 Spiritual and Moral Education aim statement for the subject and dropped all religious and moral aspects of Zambian Humanism from the syllabus content. In their place, issues such as human rights and democracy, gender, population education, environmental education, and health (including drug abuse) and HIV and AIDS education were all incorporated into the syllabus.[33] These revisions were completed in 1995 and were an attempt to respond to the *Focus on Learning* principles of "relevance, diversity, and flexibility in the curriculum."[34]

In 1996, Zambia had a new education policy document, *Educating Our Future*, which hinted that RE had to aim at religious literacy and religious maturity.[35] As such, in 1997 the Ministry of Education asked that RE be made more open-ended and participatory.[36] This saw the revision of the 2044 and 2046 syllabuses, which were earlier critiqued by some scholars.[37] The new revised syllabuses (*Realisations*) were never used in the schools. In the next section we highlight McGivern's life in Zambian RE.

A missionary teacher in Zambian RE

McGivern contributed to RE in his own ways and to many, he remains a hero of Zambian RE. Zambian RE is a reflection of missionary work in Zambia. Much of the major developments in the subject area were fostered by missionaries, long after some had retired and left the country. The initial respondents we had spoken to point out that Fr. Thomas McGivern would well be described as the Father of Zambian RE.[38]

Fr. Thomas McGivern[39]

McGivern, who spent most of life in Zambia, was born on 24th December 1927 in a family of four in Newry, County Down in Northern Ireland. He attended a local primary school and later a Jesuit boarding school of Clongowes Wood College for his secondary school education. He recalled, "When my father asked about what I wanted to do after school, the thought of priesthood and going to missions to Africa kept coming to my mind."[40] Having been with the Jesuits for 9 years at school, he thought he knew a bit about them and they knew a lot about him. He thus entered the Jesuit novitiate on September 7, 1945.

McGivern spent 3 years studying arts and science (postschool learning) and later progressed to spend another 3 years studying philosophy. He came to Zambia, then Northern Rhodesia in 1953 after being appointed for the Northern Rhodesia mission, and was among the first four scholastics to this region:

> It was on 11th August 1953 when Fr. John Fitzgerald, Br. Pat Sherry, and myself, the three appointed to go to Northern Rhodesia boarded the St. David at Rouslare, County Wexford thus making our first step into Africa, to a new life, a new country, a new language, a new people, a new everything. I went to Cardiff in Wales where Fr. John said Mass and then on to Southampton to board the Pretoria Castle, a ship of the Union Castle line, which would be our home for two weeks.[41]

On August 27, they had arrived in Cape Town and McGivern proceeded to Northern Rhodesia by train to Chisekesi, where he was picked by two Irish scholastics (member of a religious order, especially the Jesuits, who is between the novitiate and the priesthood) using a lorry to Chikuni mission. The latter holds an important place in the history of the Jesuits in Zambia since their coming in 1905. Some years before 1879, the Jesuits had been entrusted with the responsibility for what was known as the Zambezi mission, which stretched from the Limpopo River northwards to Congo.[42] In 1902, Monsignor Sykes, the superior of the Zambezi mission contacted Major Robert Codrington, the British South Africa (BSA) official at Kalomo and requested a site for a mission.[43] Following this request, the Jesuits were granted 10,000 acres of land in Chief Monze's area (Chikuni). Thereafter, two French Jesuits, Frs. Joseph Moreau and Jules Torrend arrived at Chikuni in 1905, which became the center of the Jesuit missionary endeavor in the area.

Upon his arrival in Chikuni, McGivern's first job was to learn the language and thereafter evangelize and educate. Because there was no language school at that time, he had to learn *Citonga* with the help of a local teacher trainee using a book, which had been written by Fr. Moreau. McGivern began to teach RI (which he called RE) in Grade 3 using Tonga as a way of acquainting himself with the language: "I got a primary class to teach RE through Tonga, it was true that religious lessons were taught at that time by committed Christians, pastors, priest, brothers and sisters and what they taught was related to the denominational creed to which they had adhered to." During this period, each denomination taught its own syllabus, whose aim was to nurture pupils in the Catholic faith. One of the texts that were used was known as *Catholic Teachers' Handbook for Grade 1-4*.

After the successful completion of his training as a Jesuit priest, McGivern went back to Ireland for ordination as a Jesuit Priest on July 31, 1959. He returned to Zambia, by which time the Catholics had opened their first secondary school where he taught English, Geography, RE, Mathematics, Literature, Geology and even French for Term 1 at Canisius in Zambia's Southern province. At this point in time, McGivern taught RE as a separate subject, falling in the group of those who distinguished the teaching of religion from other forms of knowledge as having its own distinct concepts and truth criteria.[19]

Although McGivern had no training in RE, he continued to teach the subject full time in the secondary school (Form 1 and 2) in 1955 and 1956. He used his priestly formation and knowledge to teach. This scenario reflects how the subject was taught in this period when there were limited trained teachers in the subject area (Figure 1).

Besides teaching, McGivern was also a prefect of cadets and regency commissioner. He later served as Headmaster at the same (Canisius) School from 1971 to 1972. His change of position and his contribution to the field

Figure 1. McGivern (Prefect on the left) on the right with the first republican president. (*Source:* Irish Jesuit Archives.)

of education were dependent on the changes, which took place in his ministry and career. In 1972, he was transferred to Mpima Minor Seminary (Kabwe Central Province), where he lectured before being moved to Mukasa Secondary (minor seminary) to head the school alongside teaching. After 4 years he went back to Canisius to teach alongside serving as an institutional rector.

He later got appointed as Inspector of Religious Education in 1982 to 1993 under the Ministry of Education. He took over from the first (White Father) inspector who had become ill and had to return to England. McGivern noted

> The word came to me through my superiors that I had been appointed as new inspector … I packed my bag and headed to Luwisha house, which was to be my abode for the next 11 years … Often times, the Permanent Secretary would send for me to answer anything to do with RE. I was an inspector for 11 years, travelling to all provinces and visited so many schools and helped where I could.[44]

While at the Ministry of Education, he expressed dissatisfaction with the content coverage of RE when he made the following observations:

> While in the office as an Inspector, I discovered that Grade Seven examination on social studies included RE, Civics a bit of history et cetera and that Grade Seven examination paper consisted of fifty multiple choice questions. I also discovered that RE had two questions instead of fourteen and all this was changed.

McGivern's discontentment with the subject at primary level led to his call for change from RI to RE because what was obtaining in the schools was still denominational religious instruction, which he believed, did not suit in public schools. His appointment also coincided with the move toward an updated syllabus at secondary level. Lane notes that toward the end of the sixties, the need for an updated RE in secondary schools began to make itself clear.

> During the seventies, Jesuits teaching secondary religious education worked within the framework of the Rugaba syllabus produced during the 1970, 1971 and 1972. The Cambridge certificate with its stress on bible knowledge was being replaced with a syllabus that emphasized education for life rather than an abstract study of the Bible. This syllabus was Zambianised by a team, which included Frs. Thomas McGivern and Joseph Hayes.[45]

The Bishops of East Africa had asked the Pastoral Institute of Eastern Africa to prepare a new syllabus and textbooks for secondary level. By the end of 1972, a set of international and interdenominational books had been completed entitled "Developing in Christ." This course was comprehensive and incorporated a contemporary approach as seen in such topics as "Christ and my humanity," "Christ and my personal freedom," "Christian life in community," and "Search and response to values."

After the 1977 education reforms, and as an Inspector of Religious Education (chief professional and technical advisor on RE matters to the State), McGivern contributed to shaping RI toward inter-denominational RE, by contributing to "Developing in Christ," which was a Zambianised version of the syllabus which incorporated humanism, Zambian Traditional Religion, Hinduism, and Islam. This saw the growth and development of Syllabus 2044 on which McGivern offered leadership on revising the syllabuses. McGivern's stance was oriented toward the type of RE that entailed learning about religion as was demonstrated in the content of the developed syllabus. This was largely shaped by his profession and the educational policies of the moment. He hinted that

> RE is not about teaching of any one particular church, but that it is an approach to each person's beliefs from a different angle ... RE is not meant to teach a world religion, nor select different religions to compare them with one another ... it is not a threat to anyone's belief and does not undermine the work of any religious body, which runs a school.[46]

Being a team player, McGivern worked with his contemporaries like Rev Cecil King, an Anglican priest, who worked at the Curriculum Development Centre to write the Zambianized version of "Developing in Christ" and coordinated the RE reforms brought about by 1977 educational reforms.[47] Rachel Masterton, an Australian Evangelist, was the mastermind behind the introduction of the 2046 syllabus. The revised syllabuses needed teaching materials and again, McGivern an Inspector of Religious Education, worked with Mujdrica to produce the first Syllabus 2046 pupils' book, which became the basis for the three booklets that are still in use today. Mujdrica recalls that:

> There were no 2046 pupils' books at that time ... when I showed my handouts for Grade 10 and 11 classes to Fr. Tom McGivern, who was the RE Inspector at that time, he got excited: he edited my notes, wrote his own notes for Grade 12 and published the first 2046 pupils' book called Brief Outline of Syllabus 2046. The booklet inspired the people who wrote the current 2046 pupils' books.[48]

He was also later involved in the preparation and publication of the revised 2044 book.[49] In addition, he spearheaded the formation of the subject association called ZARET, which had branches around the country and teachers benefited from it. The association among other things was very influential in the production of textbooks, which he describes as being another part of his work, with assistance from Fr. Edwin Fylnn and others.[49] The association helped teachers to develop their careers.[50]

McGivern thus took a leadership role in revising the syllabuses, which are in use today. The syllabus (2044) was only modified in 2012 by other personalities who admit that they were merely revising McGivern's ideas.[51] The revisions are very minor and largely consist of addition of values and skills. These ideas are not new, as Henze had raised them earlier in his *Realisations* syllabus, which was never used in the schools. Instead of the 13 themes, which were presented by McGivern, the revised book had 10 themes. When the 1996 Educational policy came into force, McGivern who had by then retired from the system but considered as a stakeholder took leadership in the revision of the Syllabus 2044 in 2008.

When he left the Ministry of Education, McGivern was seconded to the Catholic Secretariat as National Education Secretary (1993–1997). In this capacity, he again visited schools run by the Catholic Church to offer checks and balances, like was the case when he was in the inspectorate office. He left the Catholic secretariat to rejoin teaching at Mukasa Minor Seminary Secondary School to teach English and Geography. Besides teaching, he was also the Bishop's Representative at management board meetings for the Catholic schools.

McGivern left Zambia in 2011 due to ill health after being attacked by thugs. He is considered as a great contributor to RE. Many teachers of RE remember him as a teacher and inspector of RE.[52] He is also remembered as a teacher who created the bridge between the church and the government on RE.[53] Suffice it to note that it was during his term of office or being part of the education system when RE as a subject witnessed tremendous growth, both in terms of teaching resources and syllabus development owing to his quest to shift from RI to RE.

Accounting for McGivern's contributions to RE

An examination of his missionary work in different institutions demonstrated his contributions to RE, which either remained the same or changed along the way. The article observes that McGivern's position and contributions were influenced by numerous factors.

To start with, his contribution to RE was shaped by his vocation and expectations of the moment. For example, at a time when the country had few qualified teachers to teach religion in schools, the clergy were available to teach. It was also part of their work of evangelization when they taught religion in their schools. RE at the time was being used for church formation. For example, after independence, RI was not timetabled in government schools and was taught for one period a week by representatives of various denominations. The teaching could be done only when missionaries, priests, pastors, or church ministers were available for invitation by the school headmasters.[54]

The influence and contributions to RE cannot be detached from McGivern's catholic philosophy on education. For example, he applied the principles of Jesuit education to RE, which was to cultivate the whole person in terms of integral development.[55] The Catholic social teaching of the church by and large was influential, as seen in his offer and willingness to give himself in areas which needed attention (teacher, headmaster, lecturer, rector, prefect, subject inspector, and educational secretary among other roles).[56] Most importantly, he had been part of the team, which laid the foundation for the subject, and thus he took the subject as his baby, which had to be nurtured. This has been demonstrated through the continued reflections and contributions on the subject until his ill health in 2011.

The country's political and religious developments also influenced his shift from RI to RE. For example, the 1973 adoption of the socialist one party socioeconomic and political system also had its own effects on RE. When Zambia was in an economic crisis with falling copper prices, communist countries came to her rescue. In this period, Zambia was declared a one-party democracy and the philosophy of humanism took root. RE books of this period contain many passages from humanism in Zambia and show great appreciation for the United National Independence Party party.[57] Thus, all revisions and changes that affected RE had to conform to the political philosophy and educational aim at the time, which McGivern and others had to work with.

McGivern's dream of Zambian RE

McGivern's life in Zambian RE mirrors his quest for a shift from RI (which was being taught in schools when he first came to Northern Rhodesia) to RE. He perceived a kind of RE that aimed at:

> Education in Religion, improving skills of reflecting on and analysing their experience at depth, helping pupils to develop insight into what membership of faiths means in relation to their lives, developing insights into what constitutes deeply human relationships between them and others, communicating to members of other faiths their set of values and justifying them, overcoming religious prejudice, bigotry and intolerance.[58]

He also stressed that RE had to deal with religions as a dimension of life. RE was for McGivern to be taught by a professional teacher[59] and focused on the child or learner and his or her religious needs. These aspirations are closely related to the characteristics of Jesuit education and Ignatian pedagogy.[60]

It is clear that McGivern distinguished RE from RI, by calling the latter "faith development," which fostered growth in faith, commitment to one faith, and which led a person to become a full member of his faith. For McGivern,[61] faith development also aimed at deepening one's relationship to God in prayer, clarity in expressing doctrines to fellow members, increasing loyalty to one's own faith and dealing with one Church or one Faith. This is what he did when he first came to Northern Rhodesia. He later changed his position when he proposed an interdenominational approach for Catholics and Protestants. Later, he expanded his vision to incorporate the study of all religions for RE. The article argues that McGivern's shift from RI to interdenominational RE was more of a response to the educational policies in the history of Zambia. For example, Simuchimba[62] argued that Fr. Thomas McGivern from the Catholic Secretariat was nominated to the panel on RE review more because of his professional experience and qualifications as a former Senior or National Inspector for Religious Education and a sitting Education Secretary for the Roman Catholic Church than for his status as a priest and religious leader in the country. An examination of McGivern's input on Zambian RE demonstrates that his dream was yet to be achieved of developing a fully educational RE, which fosters learning about religion. This is because the RE syllabuses are still largely ecumenical in nature. This also highlights the challenges associated with the terminology used with reference to RE in Zambia. It is perhaps for this reason that Henze thinks that the title of Spiritual and Moral Education is more appropriate in Zambia though RE has become the accepted title.[63]

Conclusions

The article sought to highlight the contributions of missionary teachers to Zambian RE by using McGivern's biography as a mirror of the wider context. Whereas the focus on RE in Zambian scholarship has largely been dominated by a historical view of the development of the subject, this article delved into the life story of McGivern in a bid to understand what he did for Zambian RE as a way of exemplifying missionary teachers' work in the subject. The article advances that McGivern's contributions were shaped by his quest to shift the subject's focus on denominational lines (RI) to religious literacy fostered by RE and that these changes were a reflection of the country's changing educational policies over time which indirectly were in tune with Jesuit education.

Notes

1. Judith I. Lubasi Ziwa, interview by Nelly Mwale. Lusaka, Zambia (January 20, 2016).
2. Thomas McGivern, *Autobiography*, Unpublished manuscript (Lusaka, Zambia: Jesuit Archives, 2011).
3. Abdulkader Tayob, "Biographies of Muslim Activists in South Africa," *Journal for Islamic Studies* 34 (2014): 12–42.
4. M. Racheal Masterton, *Preparation and Production of a School Certificate Religious Education* Course *for Zambian Secondary Schools,* Unpublished Advanced Diploma in Religious Education (Coalinga, CA: West Hill College, 1985). M. Racheal Masterton, "The Growth and Development of Religious Education in Zambia" (Unpublished M. Ed. dissertation, The University of Birmingham, 1987). John, Henze, *Creative Tension: Essays in Religious Education for Twentieth Anniversay of Zambia Association of Religious Education Teachers* (Ndola, Zambia: Mission Press, 1994). Edwin Flynn, *Moral and Spiritual Issues for the School. A Paper Prepared for the National Symposium on Curriculum Review* (Lusaka, Zambia, August 25, 1993). P. Brendan Carmody, "Religious Education and Pluralism in Zambia," Unpublished paper (University of Zambia, 2001).
5. Joseph Chita, *The Role of Missionaries in the Curriculum Development of Religious Education in Zambia*, MA thesis, University of Zambia (Lusaka, Zambia: University of Zambia Library, 2011).

6. John Mujdrica, "An Evaluation of the Zambian Secondary School RE Syllabuses" (Unpublished MEd dissertation, University of Birmingham, 1995).

7. Melvin Simuchimba, "Religious Education in Zambia: Syllabuses, Approaches and Contentious Issues," *Zango: Journal of Contemporary Issues* 23, no. 13 (2000): 13–21.

8. Simuchimba, 2000.

9. Reinhard Henkel, *Christian Missions in Africa: A Social Geographical Study of the Impact of Their Activities in Zambia* (Berlin, Germany: Dietrich Reimar Verlag, 1989).

10. Ibid.

11. Paul de Nooijer and Bornwell Siakanomba, *Final Evaluation of the IUC Partnership with the University of Zambia* (Brussels: VLIR-UOS, 2008).

12. Austin Mumba Cheyeka, "Zambia," *World Mark Encyclopedia of Religious Practices* 6 (2014): 556–66.

13. Scott D. Taylor, *Culture and Customs of Zambia: Culture and Cistoms of Africa,* (London, UK: Greenwood Press, 2006).

14. Anitha J. Menon, "The Role of Higher Education Funding in National Development," *Educational Research Journal* 3, no. 6 (2012): 525–36.

15. Ministry of Education, *Strategic Plan* (Lusaka, Zambia: MoE Headquarters, 2010).

16. Michael J. Kelly, *The Origins and Development of Education in Zambia: From Pre-Colonial Times to 1996* (Lusaka, Zambia: Image Printers, 1996).

17. Zambia National Information Service, *Government Develops New School Curriculum* (Lusaka, Zambia: ZANIS News, February 13, 2013).

18. Daily Mail, *How school curriculum has changed* (Lusaka, Zambia: Daily Mail, March 26, 2015).

19. Mark J. Halstead, "Religious Education," *Encyclopedia of Religion* (New York: Macmillan) 11 (2005): 7731–36.

20. Robert Jackson and Kelvin O'Grady, "Religions and Education in England: Social Plurality, Civil Religion and Religious Education Pedagogy," In *Religion and Education in Europe Developments, Contexts and Debates*, edited by R. Jackson, S. Miedema, W. Weisse, and J.-P. Willaime (Munster, Germany: Waxmann, 2007), 181–202.

21. John Hull, "The Contribution of Religious Education to Religious Freedom: A Global Perspective." In *Committed to Europe's Future: Contributions from Education and Religious Education: A Reader*, edited by H. Spinder, J. Taylor, and W. Westerman (Munster, Germany: Coordinating Group for Religious Education in Europe (CoGREE) and Comenius Institute, 2002), 107–10.

22. John W. Creswell, *Qualitative Inquiry and Research Design: Choosing Among Five approaches* (Los Angeles, CA: Sage, 2013).

23. Colin Robson, *Real World Research* (Malden, MA: Blackwell Publishing, 2002), 181–2.

24. Allan Bryman, *Social Research Methods* (Oxford, UK: Oxford University Press, 2004).

25. Simuchimba, 2006.

26. Adrian B. Smith, *Interdenominational Religious Education in Africa: The Emergence of Common Syllabuses,* (Leiden, The Netherlands: Inter-Universitair Instituut Voor Missologie en Orecumenica, 1982).

27. Ministry of Education, *Educational Reform: Proposals and Recommendations* (Lusaka, Zambia: Government Printer, 1977).

28. Ibid., 17.

29. The 2044 syllabus is dominated by Christianity and largely taught in mission or grant aided schools. Syllabus 2046 is Bible oriented and often associated with government schools. Until 2012, it was divided into two parts: Part 1 called Life of Christ, and Part 2 Christian Witness and Behaviour.

30. Edwin Flynn, *Notes on the History of Religious Education in Zambia* (Lusaka, Zambia: University of Zambia, 1989).
31. John Saxby, "The Politics of Education in Zambia." (Unpublished PhD Thesis, University of Toronto, 1980).
32. Ministry of Education, *Syllabus for Religious Education* (Lusak, Zambia: CDC, 1983).
33. Simuchimba, 2006.
34. Ministry of Education, *Focus on Learning: Strategies for the Development of School Education in Zambia* (Lusaka, Zambia: Ministry of Education, 1992).
35. Ministry of Education, *Educating our Future* (Lusaka, Zambia: Ministry of Education, 1996).
36. Ministry of Education, *Letter Sent to Members of the Senior Secondary School Religious Education Syllabus Review Team* (Ndola, Zambia: Ministry of Education, October 17, 1997).
37. John Mujdrica, "An Evaluation of the Zambian Secondary School RE Syllabuses" (Unpublished MEd dissertation, University of Birmingham, 1995); Simuchimba, 2007; G. Karas, "Relevance of Religious Education to Our Lives," *The Challenge* (Ndola, Zambia: Mission Press, 2001).
38. Mujdrica, 2015.
39. This account of McGivern's life was retrieved from his autobiography in the Jesuit archives in Lusaka. Additional insights were retrieved from field notes of earlier research interviews on the role of missionaries in the curriculum development of Zambian RE in 2010.
40. Jesuit Archives, *Thomas McGivern* (Unpublished personal Manuscript, Lusaka, Zambia, 2010).
41. Ibid.
42. Hugo Hinfelaar, *History of the Catholic Church in Zambia* (Lusaka, Zambia: Bookworld Publishers, 2004).
43. Edward P. Murphy, *A History of the Jesuits in Zambia: A Mission Becomes a Province.* Edited by E. P. Murphy (Nairobi, Kenya: Paulines Publications Africa, 2003).
44. Jesuit Archives, 2010.
45. William Lane, *Jesuits in Zambia, 1880–1991* (Lusaka, Zambia: Jesuits, 1991).
46. Thomas McGivern, Speech at ZARET A.G.M Meeting, in *ZARET Newsletter* (Lusaka, Zambia: Caret Secretariat, 1985).
47. Mujdrica, 2015.
48. ZARET, 1988.
49. Jesuit Archives, 2010.
50. Mwansa, Paul, former ZARET Member, interview, Lusaka, January 16, 2016.
51. Ziwa, 2016.
52. Ziwa, 2016.
53. John Moore, *Interview.* Lusaka, Zambia (January 25, 2016).
54. Masterton, 1985.
55. Lane, 1991.
56. Jesuit Archives, 2010.
57. Mujdrica, John, "An Evaluation of the Zambian Secondary School RE Syllabuses" (Unpublished MEd dissertation, University of Birmingham, Birmingham, 1995).
58. Thomas McGivern, "Religious Education Vs. Faith Formation" (Unpublished manuscript, Lusaka, Zambia, 2010).
59. ZARET was a forum for discussion and exchange of professional ideas among teachers of RE whose main objective was the promotion of the status of RE teaching throughout

Zambia Zambia Religious Education Teachers' Association, *Constitution* (Lusaka, Zambia: ZARET Secretariat, 1974).

60. Mudalitsa, John, *Growing in Wisdom* (Ndola, Zambia: Mission Press, 2013), 66.
61. McGivern, 2010.
62. Simuchimba, 2006.
63. John B. Henze, "An Argument for Religious Education in Zambia" (Unpublished manuscript).

The Life Trajectory of the Finnish Religious Educator

Arniika Kuusisto and Liam Gearon

ABSTRACT

Religious education in Finland is currently adapting to new national religious and secular pluralities. In this pedagogically and socio-politically contested space, a distinctive Finnish approach to religious education is emerging which, the authors argue, reflects tensions between old and new diversities (Vertovec) in a rapidly changing Finnish society. Mindful of this complexity, and the importance of professional religious educators in determining curricula change and societal transformation, the authors use a qualitative life history methodology to assess how Finnish religious professionals view and manage such changes in the light of their own life trajectories.

Large-scale European projects like REDCo have examined in significant ways whether religious education (RE) is the source of conflict or a possible source of dialogue, with classrooms a potential locus for interreligious exchange leading to more socially harmonious and cohesive societies.[1] With intensified global concerns for urgent answers to the questions of extremism, radicalization, and international terrorism, RE has too become the subject not only of political but security agendas.[2] The study found that such tensions are mirrored in the professional and personal life stories of Finnish religious educators.

In this pedagogically and politically contested space we found that a distinctively Finnish approach to RE inadvertently reflects tensions in Finland's culturally changing, religious pluralizing, and secularizing society, modelling this around Vertovec's[3] old and new diversities. Mindful of this complexity, and the importance of professional religious educators in effecting curricula change and societal transformation, we use a qualitative life history methodology[4] to assess how Finnish religious educators view and manage such developments in the light of their own life trajectories.

Based on a small-scale sample ($N = 16$) of leading Finnish RE professionals, our preliminary findings show the Finnish religious educator coming to personal and professional terms with both curricula and wider societal change, deeply reflexive but also tentative, and uncertain. As such, we conclude that a life trajectory methodology has helped to reveal insights into an often neglected aspect of the story of curricula change, a narrative in which the RE professional is shown as a critical locus of unresolved tension reflective of wider Finnish society.

RE in Finland

An integral part of the Finnish National Curriculum, the Finnish model of RE in pedagogic terms consists of school instruction based on or around teaching groups according to the child's own[5] worldview tradition. The model presently includes curricula for Lutheran and Orthodox RE and 11 minority religions and an optional ethics instruction. Although so organized, RE is nonconfessional and religious practice is not part of instruction; rather, the approach is plural and nondenominational.[6] Nationally, 92% of pupils participate in Lutheran RE; that is, outside the capital Helsinki area, minority religions are rarely taught. The recently renewed *National Core Curriculum for Basic Education*[7] (the updated document that came into force in August 2016) outlines the following:

> In instruction in religion, life's religious and ethical dimension comes under examination from the standpoint of the pupil's own growth, and as a broader social phenomenon. Religion is treated as one of the undercurrents influencing human culture. Instruction in religion is to offer the pupils knowledge, skills, and experiences, from which they obtain materials for building an identity and a world-view. The instruction prepares pupils for encountering the religious and ethical dimension in one's own life and life of the community. The objective of instruction is a general education in religion and philosophy of life. (202)

This general description is followed by more precise objectives for the RE instruction of all RE groups. These include familiarizing the pupil with his or her own religion and the Finnish spiritual tradition and introducing the pupil to other religions. Furthermore, the objectives state RE aims to "help the pupil understand the cultural and human meaning of religions" and to educate pupils in "ethical living" and helping the pupils to understand the ethical dimension of religion.[8]

The strengths of this model are traditionally seen in that the perspective to contents is to some extent familiar to children, and through the knowledge on one's own tradition, perspective is gradually widened into understanding other views. From the viewpoint of religious minority traditions, this approach has also been supportive for the development of minority identities, and for immigrant pupils, small group RE can also help the children bridge old and new home cultures, for example, interpreting and constructing Finnish Islam identities, practices, and the tradition.[9] However, those who support the renewal of the RE model in Finland argue that it is too expensive and time consuming for the society, municipality, and the school, as (preferably qualified) teachers, (equally resourced) venues, (reasonable) times, and (good quality) materials need to be allocated for all groups. In addition, it has been regarded as particularly difficult to find qualified teachers for smaller groups, as for some groups, there are nearly no qualified personnel in the country. This, together with the suspicions that not all small group teaching actually sticks with the demand for nonconfessionality, further problematizes pupils' equality in receiving quality instruction. Thereby, alternative models have being piloted in some schools—which has added some additional turmoil into the already heated societal debate on the aims and purposes of RE.

The life trajectory study

Although many of these cited national and international studies have focused on theoretical and empirical issues related to curriculum aims and their implementation, the socio-cultural and political consequences and possibilities of RE, there are, with one or two rare exceptions,[10] very few analyses of how the religious educator herself responds to such changes. This is somewhat strange given that teachers, academics, and researchers in the subject often play such a pivotal role in not simply the analysis but the implementation of curricular change. Using well-established life history research methods, with its emphasis upon the life trajectories of educationalists[11] with those interconnected qualitative educational research approaches that put biography, narrative, and participant stories to the fore,[12] this study explored the life trajectory of the Finnish RE professional.

Research question

Motivated to uncover in preliminary ways how these RE experts—experts in the sense they are in many ways charged with the implementation of curriculum change—coped with adaptation to the Finnish RE curriculum in the midst of acute societal plurality, in Vertovec's[13] terms the old and new diversities, we have examined the following research question: "What kinds of approaches to RE do Finnish teacher educators and researchers of RE hold in terms of the aims of RE and the suitable model for reaching these from the perspective of their careers and personal life trajectories?"

To answer this question, we used a standard method of qualitative educational research, the interview, placing the emphasis upon the stories presented by interviewees as a way of understanding their professional responses to pedagogical innovation in the light of socio-cultural and religious plurality. Although we placed respondents' life stories, the trajectory of their personal and professional lives, to the fore without attempting to impose theoretical or other frameworks, the study was mindful—as were the participants—that the entire process of professional engagement with these developments had always a larger scale, a macro-political context. In this sense, even in their respective local settings, and despite the distinctiveness of the subject in Finland, neither Finnish RE nor the professionals at the forefront of curricular change are immune or can be isolated from national and global processes of nascent patterns which have profoundly affected the perceived potential roles of religion in education. This required accommodations on the part of our Finnish RE professionals' often impressively deep levels of personal and professional reflexivity. But it also brought tensions where accommodation to change within and beyond the (religious) educational system jarred or even clashed with their life experience and their expectations of and for RE. Mindful of such sensitivities the study was throughout conscious of the need not to enter into engagement with participants with anything other than a spirit of genuine enquiry in order to let their voices be heard and their life stories be told.

Data gathering

The data were gathered by Arniika Kuusisto through 16 e-mail interviews as well as two further individual face-to-face interviews with Finnish RE professionals. The outline for both data gathering techniques was the same, and the face-to-face settings thus enabled the participants to wider elaboration of their ideas and the researcher to ask further questions on their responses. The original e-mail cover letter included the same interview outline attachment in two alternative forms: (1) as a printable Word document for filling in, printing and sending to the researcher—anonymously, when desired—either through the Helsinki University (free of charge) mail system or through post (from other parts of the country), or as a reply to the original e-mail with the completed Word questionnaire as an attachment (where the respondent would be identified by the researcher), and (2) as a list of the same questions included in the e-mail body text that could be sent back (completed with replies) via e-mail. The option to return one's answers anonymously was used by none of the respondents; everyone responded by e-mail. As a research field, RE in Finland is small, thereby it is likely that all respondents would have at least recognized the researcher's name, and most of them would know her personally. Hence, some initial trust had been established already before the present enquiry, which shows both in the way of returning the responses to the politically "hot" topic with respondent information, and also in the width and depth of the data gathered through a rather simplistic measure and means. As a survey to a more general "anonymous" population, such measure would not be likely to work equally well, as such open questions are easy to leave blank or answer very briefly. Here, on the contrary, many of the respondents had visibly spent a lot of time and effort in responding.

Tools

The interview outline consisted of the following sections and themes: (1) background information (age, gender); (2) individual account on RE in one's personal life trajectory (RE related education, work history including present occupation); (3) respondent's views and personal experiences related to the main aims of RE (a) in relation to child's growth and development, and (b) from societal perspective; (4) respondent's views on what kind of RE model would best serve in supporting pupil's growth and development, and why. (5) According to respondents, what strengths and weaknesses do the following have (a) presently used RE model (instruction based on pupils' affiliation), (b) integrated RE model where whole class is taught together, and (c) would a combination of these models be a good solution? If so, what kind of combination or 'hybrid' would the respondent suggest? (6) How have their own views on the aims of RE and the RE model altered during the years? Which factors have, according to the respondent's views, influenced this change?

Sample

The data includes responses from RE faculty representatives from universities as well as various other institutions and establishments and university practice schools.[14] The altogether 16 respondents were of the ages 30–53 (average age 41.25 years) and included four males and 12 females. The sample includes professors, university lecturers, junior, or post doc level researchers as well as other RE professionals holding positions in different educational or RE organizations, some of which are related to churches or religious communities. Out of the respondents, all except one (also qualified as an RE teacher) hold at least a MA degree either in education, theology, or both; 10 out of the 16 hold a doctorate (PhD) in an RE related area (theology or education), and three others are in the process of completing their PhD.

Ethics

The study followed the ethical guidelines of the Finnish Advisory Board on Research Integrity[15] for the collection, storage, and dissemination of data gathered using human subjects. All participants in the study were adult professional religious educators, often in positions of some seniority and responsibility. These professional characteristics gave weight and authority to responses, and indeed further confirmed a sense prior to the study that there were no likely ethical issues around imbalances of power or safety to arise.

However, one especially notable emergent ethical aspect of the study was that of anonymity and in a relation to this, the safeguarding of confidentiality in reporting the findings. Thus, because of the relatively small size of the national RE community in Finland, especially at a senior level (e.g., university-employed staff at all grades from post-doctoral to professor), in the reporting of the data, detailed information about each respondent was not connected to their direct quotes to maintain confidentiality and ensure anonymity. To further ensure confidentiality and anonymity, the study was also assiduous in not matching respondents' replies to precise details of age, gender, and profession.

Analysis

Although standard qualitative approaches to content analysis[16] were applied to the transcribed interviews, in its focus on life history and trajectory the approach taken in terms of analysis put the narrative of the participant to the fore. Thus although a single interview format for each participant was used, there was much scope during each conversation for the narrator of their life story to interweave personal and professional narratives into a thematic whole. Although thematically guided by the study's core research question, the interviews, the conversations—as life history research frames them—in terms of responses were able to be arranged into emergent themes. It is a mark of the strength of the life history approach, as well as the evident topicality of this socio-politically heated theme, that these Finnish RE professionals were willing to speak so frankly and openly about not simply their academic and professional positions but their personal and life positionings. Compatibilities and tensions between professional persona and personal standpoint showed through our analysis the rich potential of the life trajectory approach. We cannot say that on the basis of small-scale study, though with authoritative voices in the field, that our analysis is either complete or final. And yet we are strongly convinced that our core research question has produced a meth-odologically sound analysis, which we have stated in our introduction; that is a narrative of the Finnish religious educator coming to personal and pro-fessional terms with both curricula and wider societal change, deeply reflexive but also tentative, and (albeit at times only) uncertain. The analysis, as for the life trajectory methodology, has helped to reveal insights into an often neglected aspect of the story of curricula change, a narrative in which the RE professional is shown as a critical locus of unresolved tension reflective of wider Finnish society. These general findings are presented, and for reasons of space, briefly here through a multiplicity of voices, mere snippets of stories, but to draw together what for us was a collective story, with personal and individual differences, through one life trajectory story—that of Paju, a unisex name meaning Willow to incorporate, include female and males voices through our one anonymized but true-to-professional-life character.

The life trajectory of the Finnish religious educator

General findings

The aim of the overall study was to examine the kinds of approaches to RE that Finnish teacher educators and researchers of RE hold in terms of the aims of RE and the suitable model for reaching these, from the perspective of their careers and personal life trajectories. The educational and occupational trajectories of the respondents typically included an MA in education and/or theology, and a completion of a PhD. In addition to this, the respondents typically hold some years of teaching experience, either in secondary school RE (in primary school RE is taught by class teachers, whereas in lower and upper secondary school it is taught by subject teachers), or as early childhood education and care, preschool, or primary school teacher (in all of which RE is only one of the taught content areas), followed by more research on RE and related themes, and then teacher training or in-service teacher training experience. Several of the participants have also been involved in developing either the national curriculum for RE in different levels,[17] or have been developing widely used books or other teaching materials for prominent national publishing houses. "A lot has changed: this has been influenced by the fact that besides merely the theoretical examination I've also examined the practical approach. E.g. in terms of educational philosophy, I'd still be a sturdy supporter of the model based on child's own religion." We find the tension evokes by this change provoking this participant to questioning their own judgement on matters of value and principle: "I don't know if I still ought to be, in principle."

The tension evoked by curricular change is perceived clearly as mirrored wider societal-cultural-political upheaval: "but the knowledge on educational field, the following of the societal situation and the deepening of my understanding on the integrated model have directed my thinking into another direction." The tension is felt as a personal and professional responsibility, even a burden: "I feel responsibility on the future of the subject (that I cannot hang myself into supporting a model for which I cannot see a future even if it would better apply to my thinking)."

To us, this highlights the societal pressures toward the RE in Finnish curricula in the first place—many of these professionals see that the main issue is to maintain the subject in schools and, to ensure that aim is reached, they are willing to give in somewhat to what the instruction could be like in the "ideal world" that can be seen from this data extract.

When it comes to the changes in their views and personal experiences related to the aims of RE, and the RE model, the data includes factors that have altered the views and opinions of these professionals gradually, though societal change and the development of professionalism (work experience, gaining deeper understanding of the needs of the pupils), or personal life experiences (e.g., extended travel in different continents). As regards to the gradual development of opinions into a different direction, many have mentioned societal change in Finland, and the increasing pluralism and the increasing prominence of religious diversity in the society. More precisely, the respondents mention that their views have been influenced following particular turning points or meaningful life experiences, such as through personal contacts or co-operation with members of minority groups (one respondent),[18] or convincing arguments by other people in mutual in discussions (three respondents), extended international travel (one respondent), or other international influences (one respondent). Also work experience was seen meaningful by many, whether at the university or in the everyday of schools (six respondents), and the teaching position including the curriculum renewals also influencing the personal "updates" in educational aims related to RE (one respondent). Furthermore, it was mentioned that one having to justify her own position to others (one respondent), increasing one's knowledge on the possible alternatives (e.g., further education; four respondents) or research on the topic (own/other) (three respondents) can crystallize one's personal views.

Several respondents also mentioned that societal change (three respondents) and increased secularization (one respondent) and societal pluralism (four respondents) were seen as causing more complexity in organizing the RE practicalities in schools. These were causing pressure for renewing RE (two respondents) and also for the risk of marginalization of RE as a subject or that RE will be removed from the curriculum if the subject is not developed further (four respondents). Thereby, one of the reasons for the supporting of changes was that the respondents' main motivation in keeping RE in the curriculum in the first place (three respondents). Finally, four respondents said that there has not been a significant change in their views about RE throughout years. The reasons for not adopting a different view during work trajectory were explained for instance in the following way:

> [My view] has remained rather similar. I haven't really been that interested on the discussion on the RE model, as it is usually triggered by structures and then the actual justifications are elsewhere than in the pedagogics. But perhaps I've become more actively aware of the importance for recognition of the diversity within a particular religious tradition and thereby seen opportunities for providing stronger support for dialogue skills also in the segregated instruction.

This quote illustrates that despite heated debate in the topic, not all RE professionals, even those in more senior levels, want to give in to the societal pressures. Furthermore, besides highlighting the fact that sometimes the professionals may not necessarily alter the direction of their thinking altogether but rather gain more in-depth elements into their perspective, this data extract is also interesting in bringing added emphasis on the dialogue skills, another much highlighted topic in the societal debate on the Finnish RE in the recent years. This is thought-provoking from the perspective that although it is an important element in the guidelines, too, it is naturally merely one of the aspects in the requirements sets for the subject nationally.

Another professional says, in similar lines:

> For me, the model is not the question, but that RE would at least be taught in the comprehensive education, and that it would, in accordance, be comprehensive. The contents hold greater significance to me than the model. Mutual worldview education feels threatening at present because I'm not sure whether they'd succeed with the [RE] curriculum, or I don't know who would do it or which instance? I do trust the National Board of Education.

Also this professional brings the discussion close to heart by talking about the "greater significance to me" as well as how the mutual worldview education "feels threatening at present"—after already initially beginning with "[f]or me ... " Hence, this quote illustrates the personal significance of RE as a subject to many of these professionals.

In the following, we will present now the life trajectory of Paju for insight into one professional and personal life trajectory through the quandaries of contemporary Finnish RE.

Paju: The life trajectory of a Finnish religious educator

Paju opens the conversation with a brief personal account on the topic by explaining his own theoretical contributions to the field, as well as saying, "And so then I've got quite a lot of the kind of more pragmatic processing of the topic." Paju has experience in teaching RE both at school and in the university level. Similar trajectories were shared by several of the respondents with a "first career" as an RE teacher, followed by research and university level teaching.

As regards the competences for global citizenship, Paju believes in RE for several reasons: "Strengthening moderate and wide interpretations of faith and combatting extremism. Bringing up critical citizens. Dialogue between religions." Paju also notes the interrelatedness of the current situation related to the challenges of RE with what Vertovec[19] called "new" diversity, saying, "This is sort of, we have, this situation derives from the short history of migration in Finland and that."

A background in theology, which in the data was often preceded by active participation in the Lutheran Church's youth work activities, as well as confirmation camp participation and later assistant camp councillor ['isonen'] duties, is visible in several accounts of the respondents' views about the main aims of RE in schools. Paju holds several university degrees, with his/her background in theology; increased educational and RE perspectives having gained importance in Paju's work later. The strong theoretical competence in theology is visible in many of Paju's answers, like when talking about the meaning of RE for the growth and development of the child:

> Everything is not ... deflated in the here and now, so what is there then—there can be different theories about that. And the recognizing of the multitude of different perspectives: that there are, in fact, varied justified perspectives to many questions, ethical and others. That it may not necessarily be taught in Maths that there are right and wrong answers.

Hence, Paju recognizes the importance of making the children think about the nature of knowledge; what can be known; which questions can be answered with a more definitive answers, and then again, which questions would gain a whole spectrum of truth claims from different traditions and individuals. He continues elaborating this topic from the perspective of an individual: "People do also have the kind of blurred situations or something. Or even sometimes the sort of issues that one cannot really choose the option that one knows is the one that should be chosen."

This leads him to sum up what he sees as the "take home value" of RE from the perspective of an individual child and her developmental trajectory: "Overall, from the perspective of child's growth and development, what are the transferable skills that RE as a subject provides to the children? ... I do think that these same aims can in principle be found in other traditions."

Like most respondents, Paju believes that current RE model have particular strengths and weaknesses. Other informants present their perspectives from the viewpoints of various stakeholders such as religious minority background pupils. Several respondents also refer to the recent study by Inkeri Rissanen[20] on the Finnish Islam RE, when justifying their views on these questions. Through Rissanen's findings, these professionals refer to the importance of minority RE in the supporting of the pupils' religious identity, and interconnectedness with citizenship or "Finnishness" construction. Referring to Rissanen's study, Paju says in the interview:

> [T]he point is that there is a place where they can experience that 'We are good Finnish Muslims'. And ponder what that means to be a Finnish Muslim, sort of a combination of citizenship and Islam. ... And that [aim] won't be reached in any way in this kind of worldview education. ... In terms of minority politics ... Educating critical citizens.

Paju thus believes that the present RE model would be beneficial from societal perspective for both the educating of critical citizens and for the fact that minority RE can work as a means of "interpreting Finnishness" into the minority traditions—and vice versa.

The informants in the study generally acknowledged several challenges in the present model as regards to its practical implementation (e.g., expense, segregation of pupils to various classrooms). Similarly, the mutual, integrated model was seen to have both pros and cons; for example, the management of schedules and other practicalities and dialogue between religions possibly more practical to organize. However, many of the challenges were seen to relate to these exact issues, for example the weakening of both minority and majority rights to one's own tradition, and the fear that the subject matter would be weakened with a more general approach. Furthermore, an important challenge was seen in how such mutual instruction would, in fact, be implemented, and what exactly is even meant by this much utilized buzz-word of 'dialogue'. Paju says:

> [T]he dialogue between religions … is the challenge of our time. And it does not of course mean that—no explicit dialogue between religions; that a Muslim sits on the other side of the table and the Christian on the other and then it's sort of carried out. … It only means that you can understand that this other person has another religion, and respect that. These are the skills in religious dialogue, although these wouldn't realize in any sort of verbal explication.

Hybrid models combining elements of both the segregated and the integrated ones, are also offered by the respondents. The following extract in Paju's interview gathers together many views also present in the other answers:

> [T]here's a problem embedded in this one naturally: what is that "own" tradition? … especially small children, the "own" the sort of "own" background tradition narrative, the knowledge on that offers this sort of a bouncing platform from where to then be able to see where does one come from and how do we encounter others. Of course it could, in theory, be done through a mutual RE instruction with a strong emphasis on the positive freedom for religion, when, if the mutual instruction principle would be the teaching of the "own" religion. And everyone would be treated individually then, even if they would all sit in the same space. But in practice it of course feels rather impossible to implement it in one classroom, directed by one teacher. … But then again I also think that the whole school culture should support the dialogue, create the opportunities for encounters also. [S]ay, in upper secondary, for example sort of, it could be a mutual subject. … In lower secondary it could be a mutual subject, but not in primary school.

In terms of the development of (1) theological / RE perspectives; and (2) encounter with religion directly (ethnographic experience)—in Paju's theoretical and practical life trajectory, there are several significant events brought up in the interview. As mentioned above, Paju's theoretical thinking derives from his strong theological foundation combined with practical experience of teaching in different educational levels. Paju mentions that university teaching has been useful for processing and conceptualizing matters related to RE. Paju went on several trips to different parts of the world that significantly influenced in the widening of his horizons in the professional sense. Paju says, "I wouldn't be the same person that I am now if I hadn't been in [country] and started [year] to study theology and sort of gone in [country] backpacking, through which I got sort of challenged; that my sort of ways to conceptualize the world were completely inadequate."

Moreover, Paju mentions co-operating with minority representatives and groups both in Finland and internationally as significant experiences that have increased his understanding of different stakeholders. Also to the fore in Paju's narrative consciousness here are how such viewpoints are informed, shaped and perhaps even manipulated by the permeation of Finnish RE by identity and minority politics. This demonstrates a political sense of what Paju is identifying in Finland with regard to the changes of the society and its educational aims through the years and Paju's own attitudes, life experiences, and transitions during the course of his/her life history and professional trajectory.

Discussion and open conclusion

Bardi et al.[21] examined value stability and change as the adjustment of personal values to life transitions. They defined value socialization as the process in which "people may gradually acquire the values that are regarded as appropriate and desirable in the life setting." Examining how individuals' values fit the new social settings during life transitions, the present study found that Finnish religious professionals point to this development. Such accommodations and adaptations are generally fraught with difficult to resolve quandaries. Finnish RE professionals found themselves between models of inclusive accommodation to diversity, to old and new diversities, and a personal sense of commitment to a lived experience of religion or secularity.

On the evidence, the life trajectories of Finnish RE professionals indicated many similarities, including those supportive of radical RE alternatives. But the dominant concern were shared, collective, objectives for children's learning their fundamental well-being, as well as concern for wider societal coherence and wider societal well-being. The decision making process here, the professional–personal accommodation, is as interesting for the researcher as it is challenging for the participant. All seem to address a critical question: How do I cohere my personal formation and presently, historically formed life views and worldviews in professional context? Many saw the importance of societal changes important, notably in adjusting subject aims and objectives to the practical implementation into societal conditions, including competencies needed for children to live cohesively in contemporary society and the Finland of the future.

Thereby, the opinion changes described in the data are very much of the nature described by Bardi et al.[22] as theoretically meaningful to these religious educational professionals. Furthermore, such value socialization in context also suggested that many of these experts would philosophically and educationally prefer the present "own worldview approach" or a hybrid model. If some regard the mutually inclusive RE as the only plausible solution for future, it is with a view to the perceived risk of otherwise marginalizing or even removing RE altogether from Finnish schools.

Important perspectives were brought up by several respondents on matters beyond the practical organization of RE in schools. RE needs to be critically examined as a scientific, secular position as such is not neutral. Similarly, questions were raised about the selection of and balance between different traditions and other elements included in the taught contents of the subject, including time allocations for diverse and divergent perspectives within and across both religious and secular worldviews. We may say that such decisions reflect the educational values and aims of society and, critically, educational policy makers. Within this context, the life trajectories of RE teachers point to their own life-long formation as teachers.[23] But the life trajectory of the Finnish RE professional provides also a rich seam of insight for the educational researcher, insightful of societal, indeed political, as much as educational processes. In a circular sense, such life trajectory research may also provide for policy-makers in Finland and elsewhere a model for obtaining a nuanced and more sensitively attuned sense of those responsible for curriculum and societal change. If the Finnish RE professional in some senses mirrors the wider tensions in society between old and new diversities, then too, in an ideal sense, for society such life trajectory research provides valuable opportunities for self-understanding, providing insights into society's own religious and secular transformations.

Funding

Funding was received from Kulttuurin ja Yhteiskunnan Tutkimuksen Toimikunta.

Notes

1. Robert Jackson, "The Interpretive Approach as a Research Tool: Inside the REDCo Project," *British Journal of Religious Education* 33, no. 2 (2011): 189–208.
2. Liam Gearon, "The Counter Terrorist Classroom: Religion, Education, and Security," *Religious Education* 108, no. 2 (2013): 129–47. Robert Jackson, "The Politicisation and Securitisation of Religious Education: A Rejoinder," *British Journal of Educational Studies* 63, no. 3 (2015): 345–66.

3. Steven Vertovec, "Introduction: Migration, Cities, Diversities 'Old' and 'New'," in *Diversities Old and New: Migration and Socio-Spatial Patterns in New York*, edited by S. Vertovec (Basingstoke: Palgrave Macmillan, 2015), 1–20.

4. Ivor F. Goodson and Pat Sikes, *Life history research in educational settings: Learning from lives* (Buckingham, UK: Open University Press, 2001). Pat Sikes and Judith Everington, "Becoming an RE Teacher: A Life History Approach," In *The Empirical Science of Religious Education*, edited by Mandy Robbins and Leslie J. Francis (Abingdon, Oxon; New York, NY: Routledge, 2016), 63–73.

5. Based on the formal membership in religious communities, if any, or the decision of the parent(s)—mother, if there is no agreement between the parents on this—with different opportunities to choose the RE instruction participated, or opt out and choose ethics, depending on the particular membership or lack of any. For example, the formal members of the majority Evangelical Lutheran Church are required to attend the Evangelical Lutheran RE instruction, although many of the families nowadays are increasingly secularized, and the child and/or the parents would prefer the "secular" ethics alternative. Those without a religious membership, on the other hand, are free to choose between these two options. In any case, and as already the parents already hold elements of more than one "tradition" in their worldviews, besides the children being influenced by other people, the media, and so on, in their growing-up context, and gradually constructing their personal views in relation to these and through their own agency, the definition of one's "own" religion in the RE instruction setting can be seen as rather problematic.

6. *Perusopetuslaki* [Basic Education Act] 21.8.1998/628, Amendment 6.6.2003/454, 13§ Uskonnon ja elämänkatsomustiedon opetus http://www.finlex.fi/fi/laki/ajantasa/1998/19980628?search[type]=pika&search[pika]=2003%2F454 (accessed May 30, 2016). *Uskonnonvapauslaki* [Freedom of Religion Act] 2003. http://www.finlex.fi/fi/laki/alkup/2003/20030453 (accessed May 31, 2016). Arto Kallioniemi and Martin Ubani, "Religious Education in Finnish School System," In *Miracle of Education. The Principles and Practices of Teaching and Learning in Finnish Schools*, edited by Hannele Niemi, Auli Toom, and Arto Kallioniemi (Rotterdam: Sense Publishers, 2012), 177–88.

7. *Perusopetuksen opetussuunnitelman perusteet [National Core Curriculum for Basic Education NCCFBE]*, Finnish National Board of Education, http://www.oph.fi/ops2016/perusteet (accessed September 20, 2016).

8. *NCCFBE*, 2014, 202.

9. Inkeri Rissanen, *Negotiating Identity and Tradition in Single-faith Religious Education: A Case Study of Islamic Education in Finnish Schools* (Münster, Germany: Waxmann, 2014).

10. Sikes and Everington, 2016.

11. Goodson and Sikes, 2001. Ann-Marie Bathmaker and Penelope Harnett (eds.), *Exploring Learning, Identity and Power through Life History and Narrative Research* (London, UK: Routledge, 2010). Sikes and Everington, 2016.

12. Robert G. Atkinson, *The Life Story Interview*, Qualitative Research Methods Series, Book 44 (Thousand Oaks, CA: Sage, 1998). Norman K. Denzin, *Interpretive Biography* (Newbury Park, CA: Sage, 1989). Uwe Flick, *An Introduction to Qualitative Research*, 5th ed. (London, UK: Sage, 2014).

13. Vertovec, 2015.

14. These schools are a part of the universities and are run in close connection with the teacher education programs. Student teachers complete some of their teaching practices at these "Normal Lyceums" which include primary and secondary school levels. The teachers in these schools regularly supervise student teachers as a part of their work. Hence, many of the staff members at these schools hold a PhD in Education or in a related field.

15. Finnish Advisory Board on Research Integrity, *Responsible Conduct of Research and Procedures for Handling Allegations of Misconduct in Finland: Guidelines of the Finnish Advisory Board on Research Integrity* (Helsinki, Finland: Finnish Advisory Board on Research Integrity, 2012). http://www.tenk.fi/en/resposible-conduct-research-guidelines.
16. See, for example, Louis Cohen, Lawrence Manion, and Keith Morrison, *Research Methods in Education* (New York, NY: Routledge, 2011).
17. Finnish national curriculum is separate for the various educational levels, that is, the early childhood education and care, preschool, comprehensive school, and upper secondary school.
18. These figures indicate how many of the participants have mentioned these issues in their responses. Vertovec, 2015.
19. Goodson and Sikes, 2001.
20. Rissanen, 2014.
21. Anat Bardi, K. E. Buchanan, Robin Goodwin, L Slabu, and M. Robinson, "Value Stability and Change during Self-chosen Life Transitions: Self-selection Versus Socialization Effects," *Journal of Personality and Social Psychology* 106, no. 1 (2014): 131–47. Anat Bardi and Robin Goodwin, "The Dual Route to Value Change: Individual Processes and Cultural Moderators," *Journal of Cross-Cultural Psychology* 42, no. 2 (2011): 271–87.
22. Bardi et al., 2014.
23. Inkeri Rissanen, Elina Kuusisto, and Arniika Kuusisto, "Developing Teachers' Inter-religious and Intercultural Competences: Case Study on a Pilot Course in Teacher Education," *Teaching and Teacher Education: An International Journal of Research and Studies* 59 (2016): 446–56.

Dialogical Religious Education in the Life Trajectories of Political and Religious Stakeholders in Hamburg

Wolfram Weisse

ABSTRACT

Nondenominational, interreligious-dialogical religious education (RE) in the city state of Hamburg is unique in Germany, where RE predominantly is given in separate confessional classes. What has led Hamburg to this unique way, and what in particular was the role of stakeholders from religious communities and politics? Focusing on the viewpoints of some stakeholders as reflected in their biographies would be valuable for answering this question. An investigation into the connection between biography and religious education can show possible changes and possibly hidden backgrounds that led to the change in Hamburg.

Nondenominational, interreligious-dialogical religious education (RE) in the city state of Hamburg is unique in Germany, where RE predominantly is given in separate confessional classes. What has led Hamburg to this unique way, and what in particular was the role of stakeholders from religious communities and politics? Focusing on the viewpoints of some stakeholders as reflected in their biographies would be valuable for answering this question. It may, for example, be important to know if the individuals concerned favored other positions beforehand, and what personal experiences with RE and religion played a role in their support for dialogical RE. Without that background, it might appear as if the current positions had always existed. An investigation into the connection between biography and RE can show possible changes and possibly hidden backgrounds that led to the change in Hamburg. Moreover biographical studies offer insight into the intersection of subjectivity and social "objectivity" that could contribute to a comprehensive analysis of RE in Hamburg.[1] The biographical perspective is therefore important, and surprising that there are no scientifically substantiated empirical analyses in this vein.

There are autobiographical studies that show a connection between the biographies of university agents and RE.[2] There are also studies that analyze the religious development—primarily of young people.[3] And we have quite a number of empirical studies on the conceptual development of students and teachers, and on dialogue and dialogue in the classroom.[4] And there are studies on key concepts for an understanding of religion and dialogue.[5] But an analysis on the role played by stakeholders for RE in Hamburg is still lacking. This deficit is all the more serious because RE in Hamburg has undergone profound changes within the past decades in which religious and political stakeholders played a key role. Their support for the development of RE was crucial for its success. The politicians responsible for education and school in Hamburg had to officially support this development. Likewise, representatives of religious communities were invited to comment critically on the curricula proposed. There is almost no material available on the influence of these stakeholders, and there is no material or analysis at all on how far the development of RE in Hamburg was linked to the personal development of these key players.

Religions in society and RE in Hamburg

The face of religion in Hamburg has changed within the last 60 years. In the 1950s about 90% belonged to the Protestant Lutheran Church, 5% to the Catholic Church, and 5% to other religious communities or without religious belonging. Currently, there are a little bit more than 30% Lutherans, 10% Catholics (via migration from Poland and South America), 7% Muslims, 0.1% Jews, and about 40% without religious affiliation. The change went from a self-understanding of Hamburg as a Protestant society to a time, beginning in the years 1970 till about 2000, when religion did not play any role in public life. More recently, there was a growing awareness in social and political circles that the plurality of religions could not be ignored, and that interreligious understanding could contribute to living peacefully in the city.

RE in Hamburg is different from other federal states of Germany, where it is mostly taught in separate, religiously and denominationally homogenous groups. Hamburg offers an integrated and dialogical approach that brings together pupils from different religious, cultural, and philosophical back-grounds in one classroom.[6] This approach has attracted increasing inter-national interest for its ability to foster dialogical encounters between pupils.[7] In it, the classroom is not just a place where pupils are instructed about other religions, but one where an actual exchange between pupils holding different religious or secular positions is enabled. This unique approach provides an opportunity for pupils to experience difference without discrimination in the school environment.[8] "Religious Education for all" in Hamburg provides a possibility for both learning facts on religions and exchanging views between different religious and secular positions.

Aim, theories and method

The aim of this article is to make a contribution to overcoming the deficit in the possible impact of key stakeholders in politics and religious communities on RE in Hamburg. This focus opens a research area that, in the future, could contribute to presenting a more comprehensive picture of the role of key players. Biographical information of more politicians and more stakeholders of religious communities could be included, as well as the biographies of school bureaucrats, head teachers, teachers of RE and, last but not least, the students. Focusing on life trajectories would provide insight on the impact of their understanding of their own religion and the religions of others.

This article draws on two theories. Firstly, it draws on "Akteurstheorie" (actors theory), which was developed in the field of political science.[9] This theory does not leave out structural components for the analysis of themes, but focuses on the role of persons in situations and processes of change. The involvement of key persons is seen in a development where norms, values, identities, and priorities are changing. An analysis of the role of such key players, including their own changing positions, can help to understand more deeply and comprehensively the general development of change and that of the change in the life trajectories. The second theoretical impulse is the newly formulated theory by Peter L. Berger in his book *The Many Altars of Modernity* (2014), where he argues for an interrelation of two streams that were considered separate before: religious pluralization and secularity.[10] He underlines the fact that, on different levels, religious pluralization and secularity are interwoven.[11] This approach opens our eyes to the fact that that there be different and perhaps even seemingly contradictory expressions of positions within both religious and secular schools of thought. The research shown in this article can profit from this theoretical impulse when looking more closely at the life trajectories of the key stakeholders selected for this article.

A case study design seems to be adequate for the field with regard to life trajectories. The main method for collecting the data was narrative interviews. The stakeholders were willing to talk about their experiences and their changing positions. In the interviews, questions were posed on religious development, experiences, and positions on RE, and future visions for the further development of RE.

Case studies

Four key persons were selected for this research. All of them are strong supporters of a dialogical RE and were interviewed in December 2015. They submitted additional "grey literature" for the research and agreed that their names be mentioned in this paper. The interviews were recorded, and the interviewer wrote down notes during the interview. These notes were promptly transcribed and sent to the interviewees for proof reading. They were approved with insignificant changes.

Overview

The two key persons from religious communities made a significant contribution to the development of religions education in Hamburg. They have been and are members of the most important commissions dealing with RE in the city and in the University. Both have promoted the development of a "dialogical religious education for all" in Hamburg.[12] The first is a Jew who emigrated from Israel to Hamburg, and became active with RE in the Jewish community, with interreligious dialogue at Hamburg University, and in quite a range of commissions in the city dealing with interreligious dialogue. The second interviewee is an Imam and a researcher for Islamic theology at Hamburg University. She converted to Islam, studied at the University and with a well-known Muslim scholar in Hamburg, Imam Razvi. She too was active in interreligious dialogue and dialogical RE at university as well as in various active dialogue commissions in Hamburg.

The two politicians have a long-standing experience and a major influence on RE in Hamburg. Both have been and still are engaged in the field of religion, education, and society. Both had been ministers of school in various governments of Hamburg. They belong to different political parties, and both have quite different life trajectories in view of personal religious ties. Both are protagonists for an interreligious and dialogical RE in their respective political parties. One of them belonged to the Green Party and followed the predominant position of her party against separated denominational RE. Over time, she committed herself increasingly to the development of a dialogical RE for all in Hamburg.[13] The politician from the Liberal Party introduced the relevance of religion into a party which predominantly criticized religion and voted for an abolishment of the subject in public schools. He, in contrast, appreciated the importance of religion and of RE.

Detailed presentations

Life trajectory no. 1

Sammy Jossifoff[14] was born on September 14, 1935, in Sofia, Bulgaria. His father, Dr. Albert Jossifoff from Bulgaria, was a dentist in Leipzig, then moved to Hamburg and got a warning in the summer of 1933 that he could possibly be deported as a Jew. He, therefore, returned to Sofia, Bulgaria. Although Bulgaria was allied with Germany, there was a coalition of churches and others who were determined not to extradite any Jews to Germany. All Jews, including the Jossifoffs, were distributed to small localities in the country where they could live unharmed. In 1948, with the creation of Israel, the family emigrated there. In 1961, Sammy Jossifoff moved to Germany to study. Following his father's wish, he started with dentistry but, after a few terms, he changed to economics. He has lived in Hamburg since then.

From a secular Jewish life to the discovery of the unknown own religion

The family was certainly Jewish but rather traditional and not orthodox, and no great significance was given to Jewish rituals. As a boy, he often played football on Shabbat, and in Israel people used to go to the beach on Shabbat where there were finally more people than sand. Jewish religion became significant whenever a crisis and an attack happened.

In school, in an otherwise quite liberal climate of Bulgaria, a boy whose parents were anti-Semites approached him with an anti-Semitic insult. Only then it did he become aware of his Jewish identity.

During his time in the Israeli armed forces, Sammy was injured. In this situation he prayed to God. There were not only Jews in the army but also Druze, Christians, and Muslims. When he was wounded, a Druze saved his life. And he himself also saved a Muslim's life when he was injured.

Although he was living in the students' hostel in Hamburg in 1967, the Six Day War happened. Several fellow students attacked him because of Israeli policy, particularly some Muslims. He defended himself. Interestingly, they became friends through the conflict. They realized and agreed that no one and no religion was perfect.

Until 2001, he was a member of the Jewish community of Hamburg. Then a dissent happened with regard to the community's ethical behavior, and he and his wife left the congregation. He still remained a Jew and attended synagogue, but not as a member of the Hamburg Jewish congregation.

From a juxtaposition of religious positions in RE via a confessional priority to an interreligious and dialogical RE

During his school days, he realized in primary school that there is, quite naturally, a good cooperation between students from different religions. In front of him in the classroom sat a Christian and behind him a Muslim. This was not talked about at the time, because it was normal. In RE, Biblical stories were told and also a little from the Qur'an. And the basis for that education was: There is only one God. The above-mentioned conflict in college was an exception in his life, an isolated case. Otherwise coexistence was very good and an everyday, self-evident experience.

He became concerned with RE as a youth leader in the Jewish community for more than 17 years from 1983 to 2000. Every Tuesday he gave courses from 2 p.m. until the evening with all kinds of age groups. Most of them did not know anything about Judaism. It was always a matter of learning something about Judaism, and starting a conversation.

From the middle of the 1980s, Sammy Jossifoff took part in an interreligious seminar at the university. Then, as he recalled, the main question of RE was primarily to find out how the children and young people from the different religion could learn something about their religions. His main concern was the religious holidays: learning about the festival and commemoration days in the Jewish calendar, which was a focus for learning Judaism throughout the year. It was not "religious education for all."

Since the middle of the 1990s, a vehement conflict took place in the Gesprächskreis Interreligiöser Religionsunterricht (Round Table Interreligious Religious Education). Among other things, anti-Jewish views were expressed. Sammy Jossifoff did not shy away from the confrontation. Again, as in 1967, it was precisely through this confrontation that mutual trust grew. And the recognition was central: Others are not different from me. And the motto became: Learning one's own religion in the family, and learning different religion in school and getting to discuss different approaches. At the same time, the group realized that "a mess is sometimes made" in all religions, which must also be addressed and admitted in order to create a basis for dialogue. This means not to generalize but to know that there are good and bad people or actions in all religions, and that even individual persons are not thoroughly good or bad.

For Sammy Jossifoff, everything was formative, nothing should be forgotten. He then said that something has changed in Judaism in Germany. In the end of the 20th century, there were about 21,000 Jews, now in 2015, there are about 110,000. But many were "inactive members." Therefore, acquiring knowledge is so necessary. He became a Jew when someone in the students' hostel in Hamburg told him in the 1960s that the Jews killed God.

Right from the beginning, Sammy Jossifoff advocated that, although all religions represent partly different positions, "religious education for all" was important for him precisely for that reason. Self-criticism is an important element for the exchange. Learning in the field of religion and RE: Acquiring knowledge but also discussing it in view of several religions. Developing respect for others but not shying away from confrontations.

Important also are viable moral and ethical positions. For coexistence in the same "box" it is important: All live in a box that has only thin partition walls. If a quiet and civilized atmosphere is to reign in the "box," all must adjust to each other. For this purpose, respect, tolerance, and acceptance are necessary. And the consciousness that others are not better or worse than oneself. Peace between religions and peace in society are linked with each other.

Central for him is the commandment of charity, which was imparted to him by his parents. He has friends in all religions but is not friends with all who are Jews. Others must be asked about their viewpoints and respect develops through confrontation. At the center, there is the reality of being human.

Life trajectory no. 2

Halima Krausen[15] was born in Aachen on November 13, 1949. She considers herself a cross-border commuter. She moved away from home at the age of 19, NS worked for her livelihood in different jobs and passed her Abitur (high school graduation) as an external candidate. She lived in Berlin for 1 year (1969/1970), then again in Aachen until 1974/1975. Then she commuted between Hamburg and Scandinavia for some years. It was possible to get students' jobs in Scandinavia for up to 3 months. She "got stuck" in Hamburg since 1982, studied Islamic Studies, Systematic Theology, and Religious Studies, in parallel with Imam Razvi. She also had study contacts with other scholars like Said Ramadan (the father of Tariq Ramadan) and others, both Sunni and Shia. She enjoyed many stays in Copenhagen and London. In 1993, completion of the studies with Imam Razvi. She was already "right hand" for Imam Razvi years earlier. From 1996, she became his successor as imam until September 2014. Since 2014, she was a scientific co-worker at the Academy of World Religions.

Turning the faith towards Islam out of an intensive religious interest

Religion was centrally important at all times in her life; there was no time when religion was not important. She passed through phases of searching and groping until, at the age of 12, there was clarity with regard to Islam. She spent between ages 13 and 19 gathering together information on Islam. From 19 to 24 years of age, she pursued intensive learning from books and study activities, always with the community. She was ready to comply with the wishes of the community and adopted an Islamic-conservative attitude in clothing and behavior (e.g., headscarf and not shaking hands with men). Her life from 24 to 32 years (i.e., until 1982): were years of study and travel ("Lehr- und Wanderjahre") Now she is externally no longer identifiable as a *Muslima* and does not wear a headscarf. She understood more trips to Scandinavia, to the Middle East, to Iran and Pakistan.

From 1993, he led basic Islamic Studies for the students of Imam Razvi. Until 1996, she did a lot of work at the university and developed contacts with many mosques with quite different orientations in Hamburg. From 1996, she was appointed Imam at the Imam Ali Mosque and did intensive community work. From 2014, she return to the "theoretical" again. She engages in teaching and studying Islamic theology and interreligious dialogue at the Academy of World Religions.

From a denominational priority of RE to a clear position of favoring interreligious and dialogical RE

In primary school, she found Protestant RE boring: "All that I knew already." She remembered doing a lot of learning by heart: the Christmas Gospel,

Chorals, and so on. "I knew the Bible best among them all." In gymnasium (high school), she dropped out of "regular" RE by the age of 15. After that, she was able to commute and attended alternately Protestant and Catholic RE. The Protestant RE teacher tried to "win her back." It was, she said, "great; brand hot discussions." The teacher was interesting because, being a student of Bultmann's, he promoted demythologization. In Catholic RE there was an emphasis on the legends of the Saints and Church History. She profited from all and was always self-reflexive.

> I walk along a path and look for that one that enables me to build bridges and integrate everything. I also dealt with questions that could have diverted me, but I always found text passages that explained to me how I could understand it all. In class, almost everyone was Protestant, Catholic, or Atheist. I also considered this thought, reflected on what a world without God could look like, tried it out in my mind. Result: There is something that Atheists are unable to answer, and they knew that. A Supra-Ontological Reality, as Imam Razvi would say.[16]

In an Aachen mosque, RE became an issue. Families that belonged to the community, including students who got married and had children, needed RE. Her approach was that children must have a context, not only learn Arabic and prayer. To see the wider context, they needed stories, stories from the Qur'an, with outlines and references to the Bible. She taught linguistically, religiously, and age-wise heterogeneous groups. She told the stories verbally and discussed them with the children. This way she observed what reached the children and what they remembered. And that way she underwent a learning process herself. Back then, her approach was also moralizing.

From 1982, she conducted primarily classes for German-speaking Muslims in the mosque, but also RE for German-speaking children who came to the Imam Ali Mosque. Her approach was cross-denominational. She herself accepted it when children asked "abstruse questions" and even encouraged the children to ask their own questions when they were "too tame." In the Turkish mosque, the Qur'an school program consisted of reading the Qur'an in Arabic—with the aim to read it once completely. Only occasionally were reasons and explanations also given. And the teachers were unable to answer many questions and did not understand when the students spoke German. For her, it was a matter of "shaking up in mosques" as far as these classes were concerned.

From the 1990s onwards, the question of a specific Islamic RE in schools came on the agenda of the city. There was a discussion on the national level of introducing Islamic RE in public schools. When this RE was introduced in North Rhine-Westphalia, she was not convinced. She had profited from first-hand RE from different religions. But she admitted, "back then, these were still vague ideas."

By this time, there were also discussions at the university in which the great differences between Sunnis and Schias caused doubts whether an "Islamic RE" could really be the solution since it would not do justice to these differences.

Since the mid-1990s there were proposals for a new concept. Halima Krausen heard a lecture by Wolfram Weisse advocating an RE for all. In response, she thought: "In that case we could also run RE jointly." That was then the phase of Round Table Interreligious RE mentioned above, in which she participated. Before that, she had only "swum along" the demands for a separate Islamic RE. She believed that the Hamburg "religious education for all better" and more efficient. In dialogue one becomes more familiar with one's own roots, and must take another look at them: "Dialogue promotes a deepening of one's own position."

Her own experience as a student was formative: "First-hand religion. Learning directly from a Protestant and a Catholic perspective. Not talking about others." How necessary this becomes obvious from the following episode. A Protestant student expressed the suspicion that Catholics drink genuine blood at Eucharist. Such prejudices exist only when people are segregated. Her key experience was that "all walk along their way together, and that does not divert me from my own way." Religion for means ways towards the good, moving forward in relationship with each other." Here it is also important to see how others move along, also Buddhists and Hindus (also, since 1987, the Kirchbach Circle). She is "allergic" against religious and ideological "Gleichschaltung" (Nazi term in order to establish a totalitarian control of all institutions).

Life trajectory no. 3

Reinhard Soltau[17] was born on August 29, 1941 in Bruchhausen-Vilsen, where he also went to school. From the 10th class onwards, he went to the Gymnasium in Bremen. In 1961, he completed the Abitur, and then 18 months of military service. Soltau studied Mathematics and Geography in Erlangen and Hamburg, and then completed the First and Second Examination for Höheres Lehramt (Higher Education). From 1972, he offered service at Gymnasium Kaiser-Friedrich-Ufer and afterwards Uhlenhorst-Barmbek. He then entered politics, and took up seats in local and federal governments for the FDP (Federal Democratic Party). From November 2003 to March 2004, he was appointed Senator für Education and Sports in Hamburg. Since June 2004, he has been retired and holds many honorary offices.

Lutheran Protestant religiosity: Identification and openness towards other religions

His parental home was Christian-oriented. His father was a Lutheran Protestant minister, the first one in his family. On his mother's side there was a long line of ministers; her father and grandfather were ministers as well as both brothers. As a child, he was often asked if he wanted to become a minister, but he did not want that. "Not write an essay every week," was his reply with regard to the weekly sermons. But he also had reservations with regard to the intensive counselling work that he observed of his father who had to look after six villages near Vilsen.

Life was determined by religion: attending services every Sunday and praying before meals and when going to bed. At Christmas he recited the Christmas Gospel along with his siblings that he still knows by heart today. But all this was not exaggerated. Rather piety was self-evident.

With the political change in 1982 with the social-liberal coalition, he became politically active. The party was not to be left to right-wing forces. He won a mandate against a former senator, and became a member of the School Committee. "School politics with sound judgement," was his motto. Initially he found it difficult to speak—that came only gradually.

He always wanted to become a teacher, but not for RE because he had only passed the Lesser Latinum and would have had to invest much time into studying Classical Languages. But he was also shy, did not want to become a counsellor, and had already performed well in math ("favorite subject") and geography. And another reason for him for becoming a teacher was the inspiration he got from his highly committed teachers. Several of classmates also became teachers.

He engaged in little religious activity, and only occasionally attending services. In Erlangen, he was more interested in political questions that emerged from the murder of Kennedy. Nor did religion have an outstanding role in his professional life. But "religion was normal;" in every service he felt connected with his parents: "Church is a piece of home."

It was important for him to look beyond his own religion. Occasionally he attends a Catholic service, saying to himself: "How nice that I'm a Protestant." With the Catholics, the "event character" is too strong for him; there are too many rituals.

Transformation from a confessional towards a transdenominational and interreligious RE

In primary school he attended RE but does not remember any of it. In secondary school that started from the fifth form, he was treated as the minister's son, and always got first grades in his school report. Here too he does not remember anything from the lessons themselves. However, religion was not only in RE but was also "dealt with casually" by the German teacher.

At Bremen Gymnasium, RE was taught by a teacher who was a friend of his father's. Here, he remembers reading Glasenapp on "Non-Christian Religions." Already then, RE moved into the direction of the present-day RE for all in Hamburg ("that was like RE for All"). It was not only Protestant but also included other religions. Non-Christian religions were more interesting for him than the Christian one that he was already familiar with. He liked very much to look "beyond the garden fence of one's own religion." This position on religions reminds him of the liberal virtue of representing one's own position while also questioning it, developing one's own conviction but not making it absolute: "Developing positions against the background of one's own limitation."

It was only later that he dealt with RE again, from some time around 2000. The Hamburg way of RE for all awakened his interest (through Folkert Doedens and Wolfram Weisse). Besides, he dealt with RE as a member of the synod. He always considered "RE for All" a suitable concept as opposed to a denominational RE:

RE for all is good. A narrow denominational view must be overcome. But not religious studies but an RE that is confession-oriented and transcending confessions.[18]

"Religious education for all" is important. The ideal is to lay a foundation in the home and in the day care center, then the plurality can be taken up in school. RE for all should be designed in a way that the children can bring along their experiences from the church, the mosque, etc. to the classroom. It is important to visit religious places because this triggers more experience and learning than would be possible in the classroom. His proposal for RE for all: "Teaching Protestant, Catholic, Islamic, etc., for a period, for example for 3 months. That would be practically and legally possible." He summed important experiences in this journey: "Confirmation class, RE at advanced level (dealing with non-Christian religions); the experiences/encounters with the religious diversity in Hamburg that I perceived as an enrichment and still do."

Life trajectory no. 4

Christa Goetsch[19] was born in Bonn on August 28, 1952. She attended a Catholic Kindergarten, a Catholic primary school "Maria Hilf," and Catholic nun's Gymnasium "Der armen Schulschwestern." After moving to Essen in 1966, she went to the municipal Gymnasium. She had a Catholic wedding with High Mass, but this was only to satisfy her parents and to get the permission from them to move out of their home. She studied biology and chemistry in Frankfurt and left the church about 1974. From 1977 to 1978, she joined a traineeship at the Catholic Bonifatius School in Hamburg-Wilhelmsburg. She was employed as a teacher there from 1978 to 1980, which implied joining the Catholic Church again. Although traineeship had gone well, the experience of being a teacher there was "terrible." Therefore, she "fled" from the school after a short time. She had a difficult position because she had been excommunicated because of her divorce and told to leave the school "for psychological reasons." She also wanted to leave the school herself, not only because of her excommunication but also because of its rejection of homosexuals, and so on.

When changing to a public school in 1980, she "left the Catholic Church *stante pede* (without delay)." From 1997 to 2008, Goetsch became MP for Green Party in the Hamburg Parliament and group speaker for School, Vocational Training, and Further Education (until 2001 also speaker for Migration Policy); member of the Petition Committee of the City Parliament (until 2001) and of the School Committee (until 2008). From 2002 to 2008, she became GAL group chairperson in the Hamburg Parliament. From May 2008 to November 2010, she was elected Deputy Mayor of the Free and Hanseatic City of Hamburg and minister of state for School.

From 2011 to 2015 again, she became MP in the Hamburg Parliament, speaker for Arts, Culture, and Religions, and until early 2016 again teacher at a school in Hamburg.

From strong identification with Roman Catholic faith to a secular position

Until her 13th year, she was "highly compliant with what parents and grandparents presented." Attending church every Sunday and often two weekly school services. The Catholic yearly cycle was formative. There was a little "May Altar" at home. She regularly went to confession and invented something when she actually had nothing to confess ("Confession with punitive measures when there wasn't anything to confess"). Regular prayers were said before meals and at night-time. Until then she temporarily had plans to become a nun.

At the age of puberty, she questioned many things, also with regard to the attitude of the Catholic Church concerning sexuality. In her mother's view, everything was a sin, she was bigoted. Her rebellion in school including throwing orange peels at a nun. It was in this phase that the beginning of a distance from the Church was initiated, and it has never ended.

During her time in Essen, she only completed an ecclesiastical "mandatory tour" to avoid quarrelling too much with her parents. Her father was in the parish council and an advisor to Bishop Hengsbach. Her first boyfriend came from a Protestant home. Later on, she got married to escape her Catholic home. This had nothing to do with religion.

Afterwards there was a long phase in which she had nothing to do with the Church. Her divorce caused a scandal in the family. After the second marriage, the child was not baptized but supposed to attend RE—not church life.

From 1997, she found herself dealing with religion through a hearing at City Hall on Islamic RE. This event that she organized for the Green Party was a novelty in the City Hall. From that time onwards events on religion and RE continued. Through this topic she came closer to dealing with migration and intercultural education. After a long time of estrangement and distance, this was linked with a turn towards religious question albeit not to the Church. What remained of Christianity in her life: Rituals at her parents' funerals and a statement by Auxiliary Bishop Jaschke "Once a Catholic—always a Catholic." Christa: "That's true."

From a narrow denominational RE through rejection of a confessional RE towards a socially responsible nondenominational RE in schools

In primary school, RE was taught by a priest. That was a preparation for First Communion. In Gymnasium, the Franciscan teacher who was "intrusive" and had a crush on her. The lessons were catechetical. No discussion of Protestantism or other religion, as "they were heathens." Up to her 14th year, she only had experiences with Catholic RE. At the municipal Gymnasium in Essen, RE was taught by a chaplain. There was segregated RE and segregated school services for Protestant and Catholic students. While she does have memories of lessons in other subjects, she does not remember any of RE. At advanced level, she chose philosophy which she found more thrilling. Knowledge about Protestant religion she got from a friend.

In the trade union in the 1980s, she encountered dealings with wearing a headscarf at work and circumcision, but they were political debates that did not deal with RE. And from 1997, the issue of Islamic RE has been mentioned. In this context, she remembers first dealing with Art. 7,3 of the German Basic Law. Among the Green Party members in the Federal Working Group Education after 1998/1999, RE "suddenly became a big topic" which was discussed and on which policy papers were worked out (i.a. together with Kretzschmann). As a teacher in the time, before she went into politics, she did deal with "world religion" but that was in the subject of Ethics that she taught. She remembers an exciting connection with Biology because "There were students from different religions in the class. When the topic of evolution was discussed in form 10, there was the issue of the emergence of the earth and the human species. This resulted in thrilling questions. That was 'great fun.'"

In public life, events of 1997 in the City Hall and 1999 at the university were formative. In the trade union, the politically and pedagogically important view on equal rights for migrants and then also RE were dominant. But RE was not discussed in a denominational but in an integrative way. As a politician, she made it possible in 2008 that the professorship for Islamic theology was included in the coalition agreement in order to facilitate the further development of RE. As a Deputy Mayor it was important for her to promote political processes with regard to RE through the Executive: "This is a situation that you don't get everyday."

After resigning from her government offices in 2011, she returned to school as a teacher where she, for the first time, taught the subject Religion. In the school practice she considers interreligious RE a "blessing for the children." In this process, children who are otherwise unable to make a contribution in class, even some with handicaps, are "suddenly ... transformed." A girl who otherwise never said anything wants to show the other her mosque. Girls who otherwise attend class rather quietly or silently, now show strength and contribute something from their own lives. Also others, for example, a boy with a Buddhist background, his father in jail, listens, tells stories, has ideas that he wants to share. There is an urge to make an input, thus also a Catholic boy from Togo who is suddenly able to tell something. With this, the respective students are perceived quite differently in class. They show personality and what they are able to do.

Conclusion

The four interviewed experts all have one thing in common: They are pioneers and eminent representatives of a non-denominational, interreligious, and dialogical RE. Against the background of the respective biographies and considering the development of religiosity and experiences as well as priorities in the field of RE, great differences in the starting position and motives become obvious. Sammy emerges from a secular Jewish life to the discovery of the unknown own religion—an active turn towards and reprocessing of Jewish religion emerges in the situation of re-migration to Germany out of a habit of formal affiliation with a secular character.

In the presented biographical sketches we find both, a mirror of general development and a motor for new direction. On the one hand: traditional Christian positions in overall Germany and as sketched in Hamburg have been changed (R. Soltau), and in many cases weakened (C. Goetsch), other religions, which almost did not count in the statistics some 50 years ago have been strengthened, as seen with the Muslim and the Jewish biography. After a period of public disinterest in the three decades beginning with the 1970s religion and RE is on the public agenda again. The Christian Churches still are powerful institutions in society and play a major part in view of RE, but other religious communities are on the rise, especially the Muslim communities, who are more and more respected in public life and who in addition to the Christian Churches have influence on RE (insofar they must give their ok when it comes to the contents of their faiths). For such a development, it is not possible to analyze the changes on a structural level (macro-level), but the biographical study contribute a lot to the understanding of the reasons and the driving forces of such a development.

We thus learn something about the different approaches, motivations, and experiential backgrounds that were important for these stakeholders in order to become committed to an interreligiously open dialogical RE. It seems central that all of them experienced a change in their biography, partly strong changes in course and breaks in their positions on religion and RE. Their own experiences with RE seem important both in the positive and in the negative sense. In the process, the changes and further developments of the positions can also show more or less lengthy phases of secularized views: religious and secular oriented positions are linked with the developments within the biography—as Peter Bergers approach stimulates—they do not constitute an "either-or identity" for a person but can follow each other and be connected with each other: Not identity as a completed construct but identity formation as a process within a biography is demonstrated by these examples with all possible processes of change: They constitute a rich resource for a deeper understanding of present positions including the question of biographical backgrounds for positions on RE.

Notes

1. H.-H. Krüger and W. Marotzki, "Biografieforschung und Erziehungswissenschaft. Einleitende Anmerkungen," in *Handbuch erziehungswissenschaftliche Biografieforschung*, edited by H.-H. Krüger and W. Marotzki, 2nd ed. (Wiesbaden, Germany: VS Verlag für Sozialwissenschaften, 2006), 7–10, quote 8.

2. I. ter Avest (Ed.), *On the Edge: (Auto)biography and Pedagogical Theories on Religious Education* (Rotterdam, The Netherlands: Sense Publishers, 2010); H. Rupp, *Lebensweg, religiöse Erziehung und Bildung. Religionspädagogik als Autobiographie. Band 4* (Würzburg, Germany: Königshausen & Neumann, 2011).

3. M. Wohlrab-Sahr, U. Karstein, Th. Schmidt-Lux, and Forcierte Säkularität, *Religiöser Wandel und Generationendynamik im Osten Deutschlands. Frankfurt am Main* (Frankfurt, Germany: Frankfurt am Main Campus, 2009); F. Schweitzer, *Lebensgeschichte und Religion. Religiöse Entwicklung und Erziehung im Kindes- und Jugendalter* (Gütersloh, Germany: Gütersloher Verlagshaus, 2007); P. Siffl, *Die Funktionalität von Religion im Alltagsdiskurs Heranwachsender. Konsequenzen für eine Reflexion über Schule in der funktional-differenzierenden Weltgesellschaft* (Hamburg, Germany: EUB-Verlag, 2015).

4. T. Knauth, "'Better Together Than Apart': Religion in School and Lifeworld of Students in Hamburg," in *Encountering Religious Pluralism in School and Society. A Qualitative Study of Teenage Perspectives in Europe*, edited by T. Knauth, D.-P. Jozsa, G. Bertram-Troost, and J. Ipgrave (Münster, Germany: Waxmann, 2008), 207–47; W. Weisse, "Difference Without Discrimination: Religious Education as a Field of Learning for Social Understanding?" in *International Perspectives on Citizenship, Education and Religious Diversity*, edited by Robert Jackson (London, UK: Routlegde, 2003), 191–208.

5. W. Weisse, K. Amirpur, A. Körs, D. Vieregge (Eds.), *Religions and Dialogue: International Approaches* (Münster, Germany: Waxmann, 2014); K. Amirpur, *New Thinking in Islam. The Jihad for Democracy, Freedom and Women's Rights* (London, UK: Gingko Library, 2015) (Translation from: K. Amirpur *Den Islam neu denken. Der Dschihad für Demokratie, Freiheit und Frauenrechte* [München, Germany: Beck, 2013]); E. Meir, *Interreligious Theology. Its Value and Mooring in Modern Jewish Philosophy* (Berlin, Germany: De Gruyter, 2015); C. Roloff and W. Weisse (Eds.), *Dialogue and Ethics in Buddhism and Hinduism*, Public presentations of The 14th Dalai Lama; Sallie B. King, Anantanand Rambachan and Samdhong Rinpoche, Documentation series of the Academy of World Religions No. 2. Münster, Germany, 2015.

6. T. Knauth, "Better Together Than Apart: Religion in School and Lifeworld of Students in Hamburg," in *Encountering Religious Pluralism in School and Society. A Qualitative Study of Teenage Perspectives in Europe*, edited by T. Knauth, D.-P. Jozsa, G. Bertram-Troost,

and J. Ipgrave (Münster, Germany: Waxmann, 2008), 207–47; W. Wolfram (Ed.), *Dialogischer Religionsunterricht in Hamburg. Positionen, Analysen und Perspektiven im Kontext Europas* (Münster, Germany: Waxmann, 2008).

7. A. Tayob, I. Niehaus, and W. Weisse (Eds.), *Muslim Schools and Education in Europe and South Africa* (Münster, Germany: Waxmann, 2011); W. Weisse, "Muslim Religious Education or 'Religious Education for All'? Models and Experiences in the European Context," *Muslim Schools and Education in Europe and South Africa*, edited by A. Tayob, I. Niehaus, and W. Weisse (Münster, Germany: Waxmann, 2011), 121–35; W. Weisse, "La religion à l'école dans le Land de Hambourg," in *Le défi de l'enseignement des faits religieux à l'école. Réponses européennes et québécoises*, edited by J.-P. Willaime. (Paris, France: Riveneuve, 2014), 67–81.

8. W. Weisse, "Muslim Religious Education or 'Religious Education for All'? Models and Experiences in the European Context," in *Muslim Schools and Education in Europe and South Africa*, edited by A. Tayob, I. Niehaus, and W. Weisse (Münster, Germany: Waxmann, 2011), 121–35.

9. W. Merkel, Struktur, und Akteur, "System Oder Handlung: Gibt es einen Königsweg in der sozialwissenschaftlichen Transformationsforschung?" in *Systemwechsel 1. Theorien, Ansätze und Konzeptionen*, edited by W. Merkel (Opladen, Germany: Leske & Budrich, 1994), 303–32. W. Merkel, *Eine Einführung in die Theorie und Empirie der Transformationsforschung* (Opladen, Germany: Leske & Budrich, 1994).

10. P. L. Berger and W. Weisse, "Im Gespräch: religiöse Pluralität und gesellschaftlicher Zusammenhalt [In Conversation: Religious Pluralism and Social Cohesion]," in *Religiöse Differenz als Chance? Positionen, Kontroversen, Perspektiven [Religious Differences as Opportunities? Positions, Controversies, Perspectives]* (Münster, Germany: Waxmann, 2010), pp.17–36.

11. W. Weisse, "Religious Pluralisation and Secularisation in Continental Europe, with Focus on France and Germany," *Social Science and Modern Society* 53, no. 1 (2016, January): 32–40.

12. Gesprächskreis Interreligiöser Religionsunterricht in Hamburg, Empfehlungen zum Religionsunterricht an öffentlichen Schulen in Hamburg [u.a. mit S. Jossifoff und H. Krausen], in *Religionsunterricht für alle. Hamburger Perspektiven zur Religionsdidaktik*, edited by F. Doedens and W. Weisse (Münster, Germany: Waxmann, 1997), 35–41. A. K. Haidt, D. Sevkopljas, R. Mufdi, and N. Abu-Dayyeh, "Im Gepräch mit Sammy Jossifoff," in *"… und wie hälst du's mit der Religion?" Begegnungen im Austausch – Reflexionen zur Ausprägung religiöser Identitäten in Hamburg, Palestine, Israel*, edited by Gymnasium Finkenwerder und Stadtteilschule Finkenwerder (Berlin, Germany: Aphorisma Verlag, 2014), 98–99; H. Krausen, "Wie kann ein "Religionsunterricht für alle" von Muslimen theologisch verantwortet werden? Eine muslimische Position," in *Religiöses Lernen in einer pluralen Welt. Religionspädagogische Ansätze in Hamburg: novemberakademie, 99*, edited by W. Weisse and F. Doedens (Münster, Germany: Waxmann, 2000), 39–42; U. Neumann, F. Doedens, S. Jossifoff, H. Krausen, J. Krefting, A. Ö. Özdil, O. Petersen, and E. Tatar, "Die Zukunft des dialogischen 'Religionsunterrichts für alle'. Perspektiven aus den Religionsgemeinschaften in Hamburg," in *Dialogischer Religionsunterricht in Hamburg. Positionen, Analysen und Perspektiven im Kontext Europas*, edited by W. Weiße (Münster: Waxmann, 2008), 29–42.

13. U. Neumann, C. Goetsch, W. Beuß, E. Woisin, D. Budack, R. Lehberger, "Religionsunterricht im Gespräch," in *Religiöses Lernen in einer pluralen Welt. Religionspädagogische Ansätze in Hamburg: novemberakademie, 99*, edited by W. Weisse and F. Doedens (Münster, Germany: Waxmann, 2000), 111–26; U. Neumann, F. Doedens, S. Jossifoff, H. Krausen, J. Krefting, A. Ö. Petersen, E. Tatar, "Die Zukunft des dialogischen 'Religionsunterrichts für alle'. Perspektiven aus den Religionsgemeinschaften in Hamburg," in *Dialogischer*

Religionsunterricht in Hamburg. Positionen, Analysen und Perspektiven im Kontext Europas, edited by W. Weisse (Münster, Germany: Waxmann, 2000), 29–42; W. Wolfram (Ed.), *Dialogischer Religionsunterricht in Hamburg. Positionen, Analysen und Perspektiven im Kontext Europas* (Münster, Germany: Waxmann, 2008).

14. Description based on Interview with Sammy Jossifoff on December 5, 2015, from 11:00 to 12:30 o'clock in the office of the Academy of World Religions. Interviewer: Wolfram Weisse. Transcript and audio recording. The transcript was promptly sent to the interviewee with the request for corrections and authorization. This was given.

15. Description based on Interview with Halima Krausen on December 14, 2015, from 11:00 to 12:30 o'clock in the office of the Academy of World Religions. Interviewer: Wolfram Weisse. Transcript and audio recording. The transcript was promptly sent to the interviewee with the request for corrections and authorisation. This was given.

16. Halima Krausen, unpublished biographical paper.

17. Description based on Interview with Reinhard Soltau on December 22, 2015, from 11:15 to 12:30 o'clock in the office of the Academy of World Religions. Interviewer: Wolfram Weisse. Transcript and audio recording. The transcript was promptly sent to the interviewee with the request for corrections and authorisation. This was given.

18. Quote from interview with R. Soltau, December 22, 2015.

19. Description based on: Interview with Christa Goetsch on 21st December, 2015, from 14:15 to 15:30 o'clock in her private home. Interviewer: Wolfram Weisse. Transcript and audio recording. The transcript was promptly sent to the interviewee with the request for corrections and authorization. This was given.

Writing Against the Grain: The Challenge of Modernism in the Autobiographical Writings of Frances Banks—Religious Educator

Garth Mason

ABSTRACT

This article focuses on three genres in life writing as described by James Olney (narrative/memory, dialogue, and reverie) in Frances Banks's writings to establish a composite understanding of her writings as life writing. Banks wrote an autobiography, educational texts, and a book on Western mystics. I include all these writings as part of her life writing. When read together all her writings reveal a person attempting to write herself into a positional response to the encroachment of modern materialism in education during the first half the twentieth. She draws from classical Christian ideas, mysticism and current esoteric spirituality.

For several decades Frances Banks was a forgotten figure in the religious education landscape in South Africa. My previous research has drawn attention to the pioneering work she did in focusing on virtue and reflexive ethics within religious education as an early developer of holistic and inclusive education.[1] In this article, as an educationalist who is mindful of the deleterious effects of modern materialism on curricula, I investigate how her writings provide insight into the way she negotiated the transition into a more technological driven modern South Africa during the first half of the twentieth century. I will re-examine some material used in my previous research in terms of the present study of her negotiation with the modern and also examine new research material. Banks understood modernism as an emphasis on materialistic values founded on an atomistic view of individuality. She believed the encroachment of modernism in education alienated the subject and was detrimental to the understanding of self as intrinsically cosmically connected. Although Banks wrote as an educator and a Christian leader, it is crucial to understand the impact of her private spiritual journey on these public writings. In the latter part of her life, she was able to bring both the private and public dimensions of writing to the fore in her essays on major Western mystics. This interpenetration of the personal with the public leads me to categorize all her writing as "life writing" because it all springs from memories of deeply felt individual experience. I will show that in her autobiographical writings the three themes of inventive memory in her interpretation of the changes in her mystical experiences, shifts in identity between her Christian and esoteric selves and an emerging new holistic narrative are discernible. Her educational writings were premised on her view that values in education should return to a pre-Enlightenment paradigm of knowledge, structured around the classical soul-based transcendent verities; goodness, beauty and truth.[2] These three qualities, she advised, could be taught via emphasis being placed on reflection on one's personal experience in pedagogy. Paradoxically, however, in asserting self-reflexivity and personal experience, she became increasingly emboldened by the mystical experiences, that grew in clarity throughout her life and, as a consequence, she was drawn toward esoteric Christianity. An incongruent mixing of classical Christian virtues with Victorian esoteric beliefs in her writings emerges as her defence against the materialistic impact of modernism on education in South Africa. The two contrasting influences reveal a unique tension in her thought between her attraction to the classical past and the allure of esoteric spirituality informed by emerging new thought paradigms of spiritualism and perennial philosophy. In this regard I refer to a dialogue between Charles Taylor and Alasdaire MacIntyre concerning the quest narrative in modern formations of spirituality. MacIntyre's point is that quest seekers make sense of the world by "tentatively embracing traditions, but also often develop their own version of them."[3] Taylor's riposte is that such a quest is a continual deferral of a cosmological framework that traditions provide. Taylor believes that meaning in modernity is "interwoven with, inventing" depending largely on "our own powers of expression."[4] I will show, through analyzing Banks's writings as examples of life writing, that she steers a course in her writing resembling MacIntyre's position of "tentative[ly] embracing" classical thought while also reinventing it in a modern context. The close connection between her complex Christian-esoteric inspired spirituality and her academic writings motivated her to find meaningful solutions to the crisis of modernity, not just at the metaphysical level but also, significantly, at the practical level of curriculum development and classroom methodology. It is my argument that, through her life writing, Banks holds two visions of the subject in tension. One is a mystically connected subject; the other is a subject at pains to define herself in an increasingly secular society.

This study of Banks's writings will show that through her life writing process of remembering her life, her complex Christian world-view was shaped via three processes: narrating memories, engaging these narrated memories in dialogue with her educational writings, and finally by extending the themes in both narrated memories and educational writings into a set of reflective mystical writings focused on interpreting the works of four mystics.

Banks's main spiritual and personal preoccupations emerge throughout her discussion of the four mystics and their ideas.

In *Memory & Narrative: the Weave of Life Writing*, James Olney observes how life writing occurs in a three-part structure by using the examples of Augustine's and Rousseau's respective *Confessions* and Samuel Beckett's trilogy. For purposes of this article I will focus on his analysis of Rousseau's tripartite structure as memory/narrative, dialogues and reverie.[5] In Rousseau's writing, humanism had largely replaced the prior theological framework and life writing was seen as interpreting life's epistemological framework based on the analysis of memory. Rousseau is driven to find meaning, in contrast to Augustine, who seeks to find or rediscover his prelapsarian being. Rousseau navigates a similar route to MacIntyre in that he stays within the tradition but allows for reinterpretation.

Banks's writings, I argue, fall into a similar structure to what Olney discerns in Rousseau's life writing with a structure of narrative/memory-dialogue-reverie structure.[6] In Banks's writings, narrative/memory informs how the other two legs, dialogue and reverie, of the life writing structure are influenced. The three-part structure allows me to divide her writing into the following categories: her autobiography can be seen as narrative/memory; her educational writing can be seen as dialogue and her later writings on Western mystics, where her ideas are expressed against the backdrop of great mystics' ideas into the category of reverie. Seen through the lenses of Olney's broad understanding of life writing, all of Banks' writings can be seen to display elements of autobiography.

The humanism that underlies Rousseau's *Confessions*[7] follows Olney's previous work *Metaphors of the self*[8], where he argues that autobiography or life writing is a genre wherein the author fashions a coherent self and cosmos out of the incoherent data of experience.[9] The cosmos in life writing, then, is represented as a metaphor for the author's sense of self and this runs through the entire opus of the author's writings.[10] I am not suggesting that Banks's writings represent a wholly fictionalized self and cosmos. Rather, I hold that her life writing shows her attempt to bring coherence into her life experience from a diverse set of beliefs, ranging from esoteric Christianity to classicism in the Greek tradition that extends into Western Medieval thought and progressive educational frameworks.

Banks's writing is classically influenced. She follows the Christian tradition of Augustine and Aquinas, who followed Plato and Aristotle's classical notions of truth, goodness and beauty in her writing.[11] This strand in her thinking is seen in her educational writings to which I will refer to later. She writes in opposition to what she perceives as the threat of modern materialism, which aims to compartmentalize knowledge and experience into fragmented units of information. Banks invokes the classical transcendental verities of goodness, truth, and beauty and harks back to the medieval era when learning and knowledge, according to her, were purer.[12] These verities were first introduced by Plato and Aristotle. They were further propounded on by Plotinus and Aquinas.[13] But, paradoxically, she also senses that her spiritual identity is fluid. As a consequence her memory splits between her Christian identity and another, more esoterically informed identity, struggling to free herself from dogmatic theological strictures. In this splitting off of identities, her life writing is more akin to Rousseau's trilogy structure, which makes allowance for a more fluid identity in the act of recall, but deviates from more radical postmodernist distrust of spirituality and subjectivity. Accordingly, Banks finds resonance with Rousseau's type of thinking. Rousseau entrusts memory to develop its own space or knowledge. Rousseau provides a possibility for the person to negotiate the modern while still retaining a pre-enlightenment sense of connectedness to cosmic presence or being.[14]

In Banks' writing I find an emerging cautionary awareness of modernity in the face of the dissipation of the classical verities of truth, goodness, and beauty. She is writing against the rising modern world of industrialization and circumscribed spirituality. In her writings there is a sense of the need to write against the grain of modern materialist values.[15] Charles Taylor, writing much later, contrasts the pre-Enlightenment sense of a porous self, closely intertwined with an enchanted cosmos. By contrast, the post-Enlightenment self is buffered from the sense of cosmos and locked within a silo self with "firmer boundary between self and other.[16] Banks' writings reveal an author struggling with the demise of the cosmo-centered self and the encroachment of the circumscribed materialist self. In the midst of this tension, however, there are traces of the more contemporary discourse of holistic values education emerging, where learning is not divorced from a subjective encounter with the world, and significantly, the sense of expressing that relationship between Nature and the self.

Paul Ricoeur's distinction between two types of identity, *idem* and *ipse*, is also relevant to Banks's writing. These two identities are discussed in *Oneself as Another*.[17] *Idem* is the fixed identity the stretches relatively consistently over time. By contrast, *ipse* is the sense of identity that incorporates the prevailing context, both the subjective experiences and the reflections of objective world on the subject. *Ipse* therefore is a fluid identity that melts and reforms itself through different contexts. Ricoeur maintained that *idem* and *ipse* identities have a dialectical relationship, which frames the connection between the identities as intricate, rather than discretely separate.[18] I argue that Banks's writings reveal a person, and significantly, a woman, writing in the context of an increasing sense of a buffered self of modernity and materialism, and yet attempting by embracing both her *idem* and *ipse* identities to establish a spiritual and holistic framework.

The three genres of writings used by Banks can be seen to follow a trilogy structure as identified by Olney in Augustine, Rousseau and Beckett's writings. Her autobiography, *Frontiers of Revelation*,[19] forms the narrative memory structure; her education writings represent her dialogical writings and her reflexive spiritual thinking is seen to be reflected in her ideas about education. Banks' reverie writings are constituted by a set essays on mysticism, published posthumously, entitled *Four Studies in Mysticism*.[20] The reverie component of her writing is discernible in her autobiographical writings, which contain descriptions and reflections on her mystical journey, and show development in these writings as her personal mystical reflections are essayed within her accounts of luminary mystics.[21] It is via the latter reverie writings that Olney avers that a sense of self within a cosmic frame becomes most apparent, however, this sense of self is emergent in her autobiographical writings.

In terms of the trilogy structure, these genres are the search for common ground, shared spaces, and evidence of resolutions between the genres of memory, dialogue, and cosmic wonder. I will argue that these texts also encode a liminal discourse when Banks proposes creative approaches to religious education while remaining within the framework of conservative Christianity. This discourse is shifting and unclear, yet provides a space for a "softer" values-based discourse to seep into an instrumentalist-dominated educational discourse pervasive at the time of her writing. In this liminal space, I argue, Banks was attempting to transform educational religious thought towards benefitting the holistic development of the student.

Banks's autobiographical writings

Banks's narrative/memory genre of writing has three foci; her youthful memories of family, her mystical memories and her recall of her memories in Grahamstown. Her autobiographical writings from Grahamstown in many ways, represent an uncomfortable merging of her spiritually restricted youth and the mystical experiences that grew out of it.

Early mystical memories

Banks recounts that she was born in 1895, the third child in a middle-class family of five in England. Her earliest memories were of her family's distinctive lack of spirituality, resulting from her father's agnosticism, which, she recalls, "in those days bore some risk of social ostracism".[22] For her father, empirical science was incompatible with an acceptance of *Genesis*.[23] In line with Olney's argument concerning Rousseau's sense of how memory shapes a person's view of themselves and the world, Banks also experienced a tension in her life between Christian dogma and sensory experience. She, however, resolved this tension in a radically different way from her father's agnosticism, by resorting to Christian esoteric mysticism in reaction to Christian dogma.[24]

Her memories of inner mystical experiences began early in life with a fore-boding and mysteriously oppressive dream-state but transformed later in life to a sense of inner spiritual purpose. The childhood experience of oppression is captured in her account of a recurring nightmare:

> The scene of the dream was always the same formless situation. Across my entire visual field there poured down a forceful rain of power beams beneath which I crouched alone, seeking to escape; but there was no way out, for those piercing beams filled all the space there was. As their downpour increased, I ran hither and thither at the bottom of one vast field of force, until, expecting instant annihil-ation, I awoke in a cold sweat screaming.[25]

Her recollection of foreboding in this recurring childhood dream bears some resemblance with her early mystical experiences as an adolescent in terms of over-powering intensity. However, the oppressive force in her night-mares had transformed in her memory adolescence into a mystical quest. An example of her developing mystical awareness is seen in her school days. At boarding school in Southport she registered for a confirmation class that was run by the rector, described by Banks "as an unusually spiritual man," who introduced them to meditation.[26] Her first recollection of a mystical experience was as a "great force descending upon me with over-powering intensity" during these classes.[27] From her memories of mystical experiences in childhood and adolescence one can discern the basis for her adult explorations into Christian mysticism and more alternative expressions of spirituality.

Banks recounts that the nature of her early spiritual journey was informed by such intense mystical experiences. As a result she did not want to be constricted in her work by Christian dogma. Instead she was inspired by what she terms Jesus' active "Sermon on the Mount ethic" of working amongst poor and dispossessed people. She spent a period of time working in the dock community in Liverpool and later studied to become a teacher at Oxford College.[28] In the mid-1930s she left England for the Eastern Cape to join the order of the Community of the Resurrection in Grahamstown. The Order had started a teacher training college at the University in the small Eastern Cape Town.[29] A this early stage of her life she saw first-hand the effects of poverty brought about by modernization and industrialization. These impres-sions would have influenced her later writings against the influence of modernity in education.

Esoteric interests

While in Grahamstown, Banks sustained her mystical search by going on retreats in prayer and meditation away from her Community of the Resurrection responsibilities. During one significant retreat with a close friend, however, she remembers witnessing her friend in her etheric body.[30]

This experience caused her to undergo a profound personal spiritual transformation and led her to explore more esoteric forms of Christianity.[31] Of significance is the concomitant development of an interest in esoteric beliefs with the advance of more intimate mystical experiences. Banks was influenced by her understanding of esoteric spirituality in her educational work; for example, when sitting on the Religious Instruction Syllabus Committee, she described the presence of an invisible being beside her assisting her in her contribution to the syllabus development.[32] On another occasion after reading about the akasic records (record of past lives in the ethereal plain), she saw a vision of herself in ancient Egypt.[33] These memories of her life in Grahamstown point to a shift in her life narrative from embeddedness within the Christian frame of reference to a more interpretive relation to Christianity-based on her mystical experiences. There is also evidence of interest in spiritualism, common to England in the late nineteenth and early twentieth centuries, in her writings, of communicating with the deceased. She expresses an interest in the writings of Sir Oliver Lodge and Reverend Vale Owens concerning evidence of the afterlife and communications with the deceased.[34] These esoteric beliefs, although recounted in her autobiography, tended to not be revealed in her educational writings. The interest in esoteric beliefs, however, became more integral to her core belief framework in Grahamstown. In this regard Alasdair MacIntyre's observation of quest narrative in modern formations of spirituality is pertinent. His point that modern the seeker make sense of the world by tentatively embracing old traditions, by offering new versions of them. Her understanding of Christian mysticism was shaped by contemporary spiritual influences.

As her mystical experiences developed in clarity through her life, so did her resolve to express her mystical understanding in writing. Mysticism became a major theme in her writing giving purpose to her life. Mystical experiences seemed, in her understanding, to relate to her soul's journey and the life choices she was making to assist its development. As a result of her mystical experiences, Banks believed that the soul needed to be released from its earthly bondage. This idea strongly influenced her educational thinking, where she advocated that students should be seen as soul-centered rather than deficient in various ways.[35] These ideas of soul-centered growth and non-materialist values become, not only the central motif in her life-writing, but also her lessons on how to live spiritually in the modern world.

Grahamstown: Memories of a spiritual journey

Banks worked in the Training College in Grahamstown for 25 years and was the Principal of the College for 14 years. But her spiritual journey was a complex one, requiring shifting identities that pulled in various directions as moral educator, a dedicated nun and mystical explorer. These tensions were evident early on as an educator and nun, when she decided to follow a spiritual life in a religious community. In the days before her ordination, she remembers experiencing severe doubts concerning her decision. This doubt increased over the years of her involvement with the Community of the Resurrection Order, as her ambivalence toward the strictures of belief grew.[36] In the later years of her membership of the Order, when she was Principal of the Teacher Training College, she recollects befriending an unnamed visiting lecturer and started reading alternative spiritual literature. This is the same person whom Banks would later mystically "see" in etheric form. Her search for inner spiritual strength and guidance had already led her to adapt the Biblical Education discourse of the day, in her contribution to the Agreed Cape Syllabus for Religious Instruction, into an experience-based curriculum. Her educational writings are testament to her ability to straddle fluid identities within and exterior to dogmatic Christianity, similar to Ricoeur's description of the *ipse identity* "involves a dialectical complementarity … namely the dialectic of self and the other than self."[37] Ultimately these influences enabled her to develop a holistic student-centered approach to religious studies at school level, as will be shown in the following section. I will now explicate how her fluid identities enabled her to development of a holistic and counter modern paradigm in her educational writings.

Dialogue: Educational writings

The dialogical form of Banks's writing is found in her attempt to knit together personal narrative into public discourse. In these texts, Ricoeur's sense of dialectically related identities becomes germane. *Idem* identity anchors her personal memory narrative identity, whereas her *ipse* identity roves into the public domain. This is, however, an uneasy dialectical relationship because the public domain of encroaching modernity conflicts with her private mystically-based identity. Ricoeur's theoretical framework does not explain her motivation to write against modernity. In this regard Talal Asad in his book, *Formations of the Secular*,[38] offers a plausible explanation. Asad recognizes the importance of discomfort in spurring people to create their identities. He draws from Susan Wolf, who asserts, rather than the desire to form the self, the need to have a sane response to the world. The drive for sanity articulates a need to 'be connected in a certain way' to the world. Rather than resisting the world, Asad avers that the pursuit of a sane response to the world is a practical response by accumulating probable ways of knowing, instead of accepting conventional assumptions in order for the world to be psychologically and emotionally meaningful for the person. The probable knowledges accommodate the discomfort felt in the present, rather than repress them.[39] Banks's dialogical writings should be read in terms of these criteria, a fluid identity driven by emotional discomfort. Although her writings are motivated by discomfort with modernity, there is a distinct blind-spot in her thinking regarding the inequity of racially divided classrooms, although she did teach at black teacher training colleges throughout South Africa as part of her community development program.[40]

Banks' educational thinking portray the three influences of interpreting memory: fluid identity between Christian dogma and esoteric spirituality and her negotiations between pre- and post-Enlightenment thinking are all evident in her educational writings. The co-existence of these strands reinforces the dialogical nature of her educational writings. The result of these influences on Banks' educational writing is a liminal discourse focusing on the development of self-reflexivity and creatively resonant students within a living cosmos. This discourse emerges as a resistant voice against the materialist focus of the syllabus of the day, according to Banks. Banks wrote in *A Plea for Investigation of the Principles of Religious Education* of the delimited role of religion in modern society,

> The most men have done (although a better hope was almost realized in mediaeval times) has been to departmentalize their Christianity, and, especially in these scientific days, keep it to themselves as something of merely individual choice, however precious. *Corporate expression of the body politic* has only been permissible in so far as religion could be kept within the limits of agreed formulae in the strictly Pharisaic spirit. (italics added for emphasis)[41]

By contrast to the "buffered spirituality," as noted by Taylor, which Banks perceived in modern society as the "corporate expression of the body politic" that alienated the spiritual subject, she was able to inscribe her educational writings with her mystical understandings and a wider grasp of spirituality than mere doctrinal matters and holistic presentation of the student in the modern world. But because of the strong classical influence and because of her sense of the cosmo-centered student, her writing had a strong mediaeval Christian influence. For Banks, therefore, classical education was at the core of the values of education, which informed her thoughts on religious education. But paradoxically her yearning for a return to classical virtues was fed by an interest in alternative spirituality and esoteric expressions of Christianity.

Banks articulated a need to uphold a pre-Enlightenment, cosmo-centered world view. At the center of pedagogy was the soul-centered child.[42] As such children could not be molded into instruments for the technological society. Rather students needed to trust and learn to be themselves. In focusing on the soul-centered student, Banks maintained teachers would connect with something permanent in the child.[43] Teachers should "teach the whole person, not in spite of it," she wrote.[44] Banks contended that development of the whole, soul-centered person implies a seamless connection between self, other and cosmos, expressed in the values of justice, caring, creativity and compassion.[45]

Such thinking stood in resistance to the idea of education serving the materialistic needs of the economy.

Banks's emphasis on cosmo-centricity in education emerged from her defence of classical values. Her concept of holistic education was founded on the sublime verities of beauty, truth and goodness, which, she maintained, were deep requirements for the psyche. As I argued in a previous article, Banks "maintained that social values had lost touch with these deeper structures of the human psyche and that, along with Christianity, the 'psyche needed to be rescued from private life'. All learning should be based on the need of the psyche for these three eternal values."[46] An exploration of Banks's understanding of these three values as deep psyche qualities reveals a holistic sense of the self inextricably connected to the cosmos. She clearly was railing against the notion of a private self that is sequestrated from the larger environment and cosmos.

For Banks, beauty was an indelible aspect of the learning process. Beauty is closely connected to the meditative practices of self-reflection, creative writing and observing nature. A crucial part of classroom activity, according to Banks, is diary writing, recording meaningful experiences, dreams and observations of nature. She explained that the importance of such interior reflections on self and the world was that it brings students into contact with their soul.[47]

According to Banks, self-reflexive activity develops in students a sense of truth. Such activity nurtures in students the desire to pursue truth. Banks did not hold to a relativistic notion of truth. Truth, for her, is experienced. Book learning needs to be verified through the personal thinking process. Students should be taught that they are an intrinsic part of a unified God-centered universe and as such truth as a lived experience.[48] She wrote,

> We must, then, lead our pupils on a genuine acquisition of relevant knowledge [through experience], and follow up with a great cutting away of the dead wood of useless lumber, in every subject on the curriculum from Arithmetic onwards, making all acquisitions fit for their developing experience … of the young.[49]

The mystical identity found in her memory/narrative discourse informs that values in her dialogical writings. For Banks, in her educational writings moral consciousness cannot be separated from her understanding of truth which is very influenced by Plato's Forms. I will return to this point in my analysis of the reverie section of her writings. Goodness is related to the powerful influence of the ethic of the Sermon on the Mount on her practical morality. She believed that modern Christianity had "lost touch with the deeper structures of the human psyche" from whence originate our morality. As a consequence Christianity had become a mere set of dogmatic statements of belief and morality. She argued instead that Christianity is a practical religion which employed deeply set psychological concepts of goodness, truth, and beauty to navigate daily life, reminiscent of Augustinian thought.[50]

Despite dabbling in esoteric spirituality, Banks never diverged from her basic Christian orientation to education. Drawing on Medieval thinkers and values, such as Aquinas, she combined classical and Christian influence in writing. Her sense of a presence or being in her life was a defining influence that situated her within a mystically interconnected cosmos.[51] In her personal life this sense of presence took an esoteric shape, but in her academic writing she did not stray from the mediaeval sense of Being, which is rooted in Christian beliefs. She contended that Christianity as a school subject with emphasis on practice and study.[52] Other religions could be taught to more mature students, but only within a framework of 'progressive faith towards Christianity'.[53] In writing against the grain of her contemporary educational thought, she reverted back to classical Christian ideas and values. Banks found depth and richness in this thought to combat the emerging instrumentalist thinking in modern education.

Her educational writings also combined classical Christian ideas with esoteric ideas of spirituality as an interior experience rather than any notion of objective creed-based religion. These esoteric ideas found expression in her contribution to the writing of the Cape Agreed Religious Instruction syllabus. She writes that religious instruction should foster "inner development which opens the channels of awareness," rather than focusing on formulaic orthodox beliefs, which can only reflect a dead language to students. Learning for Banks should create "an immediacy of awareness of context and state of mind."[54] The goal of the syllabus was to rescue students from the prevailing "shrunken consciousness" of the age and build a collective awareness of the soul's development and a "boundless consciousness."[55] This is achieved through teaching an extended notion of the Kingdom of God from home, within one's neighborhood and outwards.[56] All religious instruction should be based on meditation and prayer.[57]

I have classified Banks's educational writings in terms of Olney's life writing trilogy structure as dialogical writings because there is a combination of her narrative memory with her public educational texts. There is a fluid intertextuality between these texts because she wrote her autobiography after her retirement from education. But they reveal the imprints of her memories of her life. These memories would have influenced her educational writings and would have developed further until she penned in her autobiography in later life. Her autobiography, *Frontiers of Revelation*, was published in 1962. It was her penultimate publication. Her final publication was *Four Studies in Mysticism*.[58] It is to this text that I now turn.

Reverie writings

Banks's book *Four Studies in Mysticism* was the last book she wrote before her death in 1965. The book was posthumously published in 1967. It is an interesting study in that it represents a good representation of what Olney referred to as reverie writing in his tripartite structure of life writing based on Rousseau's *Confessions*, whereas Banks framed her dialogical writings within a context of exercising a fluid identity motivated by existential discomfort with the modern world she inhabited. In her reverie writings I argue that Banks reveals a more unified identity as she pulls together the strands of her identity by reflecting on four mystics that span classical medieval and modern eras. By developing linking narratives between the works of these mystics, she was able to establish her own myth of her life as a modern mystical explorer. In *Four Studies in Mysticism*, Banks extended her earlier life writings in the form of narrative memory and dialogical engage of these personal narratives into her public persona as an educationalist, into the realm of metaphysical speculation. The thematic arcs of classical values, esoteric concerns, such as psychic phenomena, and medieval Christianity are brought together in this most philosophical/theological form of her life writing. Her concerns about the debilitating effect of modernity's materialistic education should be contrasted with these four essays that, I maintain, articulate her view of life and defense against modern materialism and belief in technological progress. Drawing from C. G. Jung, Olney writes that the self "is a process rather than a settled state of becoming," this becoming is present to the sense of the whole universe. "Only with the coming of death must the self settle its accounts" with its life. In this state of dawning finality, Banks uses her exploration of Western mystics as a medium to explore and craft a final sense of self in relation to the infinite expanse of the cosmos.[59] Banks's concerns regarding modernity are written into her studies of the four mystics as she draws out classical and esoteric ideas in these mystics' ideas. She considers St Theresa of Avila, St John of the Cross, Plotinus, and Pierre Teilhard de Chardin in the book and when read in unison they become a metaphor for her life explorations in modernity.

Banks began her study of mysticism by focusing on St Theresa of Avila. Her interest in psychic phenomena and "visions" was evident in her appraisal of St Theresa. She referred to St Theresa as a "sensitive' and provided examples from the mystics' writings which she considers to be evidence of psychic powers.[60] When Banks believed she saw the ethereal body of her friend it marked an important turning point in her life toward linking such ethereal visions to her life-long mystical experiences. She perceived the same link between psychic phenomena and the mystical path in St Theresa's writings. Banks highlighted the instances in St Theresa's writings which, for her, indicate clairvoyance and clairaudience. She wrote of being carried to heaven and seeing her father and mother, and seeing a departed nun.[61] She also recounted experiences of psychic attack from devils.[62] As St Theresa journeys through the mystical mansions of her *Interior Castle* her senses become more refined, until Banks described how St Theresa enters into a spiritual betrothal with Spirit in a celestial union. Banks is drawn to St Theresa's sensory description of this union as, "rain falling from heaven,"[63] reminiscent of her own mystical experiences as an adult. The recollection of later mystical experiences is strikingly similar. Banks described her adult mystical experiences as "formless and unemotional, inspiring and immeasurably refreshing. It had a crystalline spiritual quality, unlike the heavy-laden down-pour of the early days.

In St John of the Cross's writings, Banks observes his association between intellectual interest in Neoplatonism with his soul's contemplation of God.[64,65] In the attention drawn to this association, Banks revealed her own concern in linking classical thought to Christianity in her own writing. She described the importance of the rational mind in St John's writings, which needs to operate in tandem with orthodox religious practice and 'affective-intuitive or experiential urges.[66] In drawing out these elements in St John's writings there is evidence of Banks attempting to reconcile these three elements in her own writing. Indeed, in the concluding paragraphs of the chapter on St John, Banks asserted

> At the junction point between the pagan and the Christian worlds, in the the century of our era, a perennial philosophy grounded upon a synthesis of ancient spiritual foundations was given definition through spoken word and the written word by one of the greatest philosophers of all times, namely Plotinus. And it was upon this four-square platform of Neoplatonism that Christianity built its own vast edifice of doctrinal philosophy, and notably medieval scholasticism.[67]

It is the study and re-interpretation of these thinkers within a modern framework that Banks pins her hope of of negotiating a path through modernity. St Augustine was a Neo-Platonist before his conversion to Christianity. Much of Plotinus's teaching echoes Christian beliefs. For example, wrote Banks, "that the object of life for Plotinus was to bring souls backs to 'their Heavenly Father' or to unite with 'Divine in the universe."[68,69] Banks goes as far as to argue that modern spiritual meditation lends itself from Plotinus. Banks is arguing here that not only Christianity, but most forms of spiritual practice derive from Plotinus, whether acknowledged or not. Indeed whether Christian or not Banks avers, based on her reading of Plotinus, that all humanity in reality is spirit.[70] The good, the beautiful, and the true are earthly reflections of the unity of love in the Great spirit or universal Soul.[71] Hence the love of the triad of beauty, truth, and the good forms a conduit to their prototypes in the spiritual world.[72] The linking of higher souls to lower souls, reaching to the universal soul occurs through group activity between souls forming interlinking group structures. In a concluding note concerning Plotinus's huge influence on Western mysticism Banks cites Evelyn Underhill who maintains that Plotinus provides the framework for Christian mysticism along with non-Christian (pagan) forms of mysticism.[73] Based on this assertion, Banks maintains that modern Christianity needs to reassert its indelible connection to neo-Platonism. In addition, for Banks, modern Christianity, and its true neo-Platonist roots, can be substantiated by science.[74] This latter avowal leads Banks to consider the modern mystical paleontology of Pierre Teilhard de Chardin.

De Chardin's mystical theory was that the activity of the Universal soul could be traced from primal matter through the evolution of physical life organic life up to hominization of the planet and spirit.[75] In the hominization of spirit it begins to be able to reflect on itself and know that one knows. De Chardin called this the Noosphere.[76] He argued that the earth acquired a new skin and discovered its soul.[77] In stating the latter Banks reminds her reader that de Chardin is echoing Plotinus's dictum that "humans can know the unknowable because we are the unknowable.[78] Banks wrote that according to de Chardin all life is linked in the divine milieu. However, to realize this mystical state of unity Banks draws attention to de Chardin's point that Christianity must move away from Mediterranean Christianity and orthodoxy. Science, Christianity, and modern man 'must be guided by his inner vision'.[79] The universe in essence is a personal universe.[80] However de Chardin maintains that the Omega point of spiritual discovery can only be achieved via group activity, again echoing Plotinus—a point that Banks lures out of de Chardin's writings.[81]

Conclusion

In this article I have analyzed Frances Banks's writings in terms of Olney's tripartite life writing structure of narrative/memory, dialogue, and reverie to foreground mystical influences in her educational writings. These mystical influences, both in classical and esoteric thought, provide a means for her to safeguard education—and religious education in particular—against material-ism and modern instrumentalist views of the subject. I have focused on the inter-relationship between Olney's trilogy structure in Banks' writings between her autobiography, educational writings and her essays on Christian mystics. In particular I looked at the development of her mystical ideas and experiences in her autobiography, *Frontiers of Revelation*, and how these ideas and experiences influenced her educational writings, with special reference to her soul-driven educational approach and her revolutionary ideas on group work in the classroom. I explored how these ideas were further developed in the reverie component of her auto/biographical writing in bringing together her life's writings and ideas essayed into her reflections on the Western mystical tradition. I endeavored to explain her ambiguous writings, containing both an adherence to classical ideas and modern esoteric spiritu-ality, within the trilogy structure. Despite the fact that her private spirituality moved away from orthodox Christianity towards 'esoteric' Christianity, she wrote these ideas, developed from her life memories, into her educational writings. She argued that education should be appropriate to the experiences of young people. By applying Olney's trilogy structure to life writing, I determine that Banks's revolutionary educational ideas can be explained in terms of her resistance to what she perceived as the increasingly instrumentalist approach to education during the period when she was writing. In so doing she argued for the retention of the classical approach to education, which was upheld by three pillars of truth, beauty, and goodness. Yet it is the multiple voices in the trilogy structure of life writing, which Olney observes, which makes Banks's life writing so intriguing. This retroactive aspect of life writing, which harks back to an earlier mediaeval understanding of Christianity, is contradictory to her more innovative educational thinking and modern esoteric spirituality. The multiple identities in Banks' life writing bring conflict, but also innovation, which presaged the growth of contemporary holistic education. Ultimately her multiple identities in the trilogy of her life writing led to the development of a liminal discourse in resistance modern instrumentalist encroachments into education at that time.

Funding

Funding was received from the University of South Africa.

Notes

1. Garth Mason, "Frances Banks—Mystic and Educator: The Visionary Solipsist," *Alternation: Interdisciplinary Journal for the Study of Arts and Humanities in Southern African* 11 (2013): 63.
2. Plotinus, *The Enneads* (London, UK: Penguin Classics, 1991), 45, 347 and 365.
3. Charles Taylor, *Sources of the Self: Making of the Modern Identity* (Cambridge, UK: Cambridge University Press, 1992), 17.
4. Taylor, 1992, 18.
5. James Olney, *Memory and Narrative: The Weave of Life-writing* (Chicago, IL: University of Chicago, 1998).
6. Jean-Jacques Rousseau, *The Confessions* (London, UK: Penguin Classics, 1954), 7–11.
7. Rousseau1954, 7.
8. James Olney, *Metaphors of the Self: The Meaning of Autobiography* (Princeton, NJ: Princeton University Press, 1972).
9. Olney, 1972, 4 and 11.
10. Olney, 1972, 6.
11. Bertrand Russell, *History of Western Philosophy* (London, UK: George Allen and Unwin, 1947), 150, 152, 191, and 484.
12. Frances Banks, "A Plea for Investigation of the Investigation of the Principles of Religious Education," *Christian Council Study Series* 5 (1943): 4.
13. Russell, 1947, 150, 152, 191,312 and 484.
14. Olney, 1998, 110.
15. Banks, 1943, 4.
16. Website: "The Immanent Frame: Secularism, Religion, and the Public Sphere," http://blogs.ssrc.org/tif/2008/09/02/buffered-and-porous-selves/ (accessed 27 February 2016).

17. Paul Ricoeur, *Oneself as Another* (Chicago, IL: University of Chicago, 1994), 3.
18. Ricoeur, 1994, 4.
19. Frances Banks, *Frontiers of Revelation* (London, UK: Parrish Publishers, 1962).
20. Frances Banks, *Four Studies in Mysticism* (Lincolnshire, UK: Mysticism Committee of the Churches Fellowship for Psychical and Spiritual Studies, 1967).
21. Banks, 1962, 7 and 27.
22. Banks, 1962, 5.
23. Banks, 1962, 5.
24. Mason, 2013, 164.
25. Banks, 1962, 6.
26. Banks, 1962, 6.
27. Banks, 1962, 6.
28. Banks, 1962, 11.
29. Banks, 1962, 27.
30. Banks, 1962, 27.
31. Banks, 1962, 44.
32. Banks, 1962, 25.
33. Banks, 1962, 29.
34. Banks, 1962, 7.
35. Frances Banks, *Educating Towards a Christian Society* (London, UK: Church Education Publication, 1943), 28.
36. Banks, 1962, 17.
37. Ricoeur, 1994, 2–3.
38. Talal Asad, *Formations of the Secular: Christianity, Islam, Modernity* (Stanford, CA: Stanford University Press, 2003).
39. Asad, 2003, 73.
40. Banks, 1962, 124.
41. Banks, 1943, 4.
42. Banks, 1943, 19.
43. Banks, 1943, 28.
44. Banks, 1943, 31.
45. Banks, 1943, 24.
46. Banks, 1943, 10; Mason, 2013, 175.
47. Banks, 1943, 46.
48. Banks, 1943, 52–54; Mason, 2013, 176.
49. Banks, 1943, 54.
50. Banks, 1943, 55–56.
51. Banks, 1943, 57 and 61.
52. Banks, 1943, 61.
53. Banks, 1943, 71.
54. Mason, 2013, 176.
55. Mason, 2013, 183.
56. Mason, 2013, 183.
57. Mason, 2013, 184.
58. Frances Banks, 1967.
59. Olney, 1972, 6.
60. Frances Banks, 1967, 14.
61. Frances Banks, 1967, 6.
62. Frances Banks, 1967, 8.
63. Frances Banks, 1967, 8.

64. Frances Banks, 1962, 27.
65. Frances Banks, 1967, 17.
66. Frances Banks, 1967*dies*, 23.
67. Frances Banks, 1967, 24.
68. Frances Banks, 1967, 27.
69. Plotinus, 1991, 443.
70. Frances Banks, 1967, 29.
71. Frances Banks, 1967, 30.
72. Frances Banks, 1967, 35.
73. Frances Banks, 1967, 39.
74. Frances Banks, 1967, 40.
75. Frances Banks, 1967, 44–47.
76. Pierre Teilhard De Chardin, *The Phenomenon of Man* (London, UK: Collins,1966), 191.
77. Frances Banks, 1967, 48.
78. Frances Banks, 1967, 48.
79. Frances Banks, 1967, 52.
80. Frances Banks, 1967, 53.
81. Frances Banks, 1967, 54.

Continuity and Change: Experiences of Teaching Religious Education in the Light of a Life Trajectory of Hifz and Secular Education

Jenny Berglund

ABSTRACT

In this article, microhistory is used to (1) bring understanding to some of the educational, but also social and political questions that at present surround Muslims schools and Islamic Education in England; and (2) to question oft created dichotomy between Islamic and secular education, by bringing forward an educational journey, consistent of both Islamic education and secular education. The focus lies on the life of a British hafiz who works as a religious education teacher at a Muslim school in East London.

In his keynote lecture at the International Association for the History of Religions (IAHR) congress in Erfurt 2015, professor Abdulkader Tayob pointed out that microhistory constituting religiosity is a neglected field within the study of religions but that the genre of biography historically is well established. Whereas biography focuses on the unique life of an individual, usually someone who has made a significant contribution to history, microhistory points to the significance of a life in the light of the general religious, social, or political history in question. Lepore stated in her well-known article "Love Too Much; Reflections on Microhistory and Biography" that "however singular a person's life may be, the value of examining it lies not in its uniqueness, but in its exemplariness, in how that individual's life serves as an allegory for broader issues affecting the culture as a whole."[1]

In this article there is not space to fully encompass the genre of microhistory. My intention is instead to focus aspect of religiosity and education in the life of a British hafiz[2], here called Ibrahim, who works as a religious education (RE, here meaning world religions) teacher at a Muslim school in East London.[3] I do this to (1) bring understanding to some of the educational, but also social and political questions that at present surround Muslims schools and Islamic Education in England and (2) to question oft created dichotomy between Islamic and secular education, by bringing forward his educational journey, consistent of both Islamic education and secular education, as well as his recent career as a teacher.[4]

Ibrahim

Ibrahim is in his mid 30ies and teaches RE, in a Muslim boys school in East London. The school is a Year 7–11 school with around 70 students. Ibrahim, as several of the teachers at the school, is a *hafiz*, "one who remembers" (i.e., a guardian of the Quran).[5] Although Ibrahim is a hafiz, he does not teach the hifz classes at the Muslim school. Instead, as already mentioned, he teaches RE as well as some secular subjects. Tafiz/hifz thus makes up an important element at the Muslim school. The first hours of each school day is spent on reading, reciting, and memorizing the Quran. If you enter the school between 8 a.m. and 9.45 a.m., the school building is filled by what Ibrahim describes as a "warm buzz" of boys' voices who recite the Quran.[6] What distinguishes Ibrahim from several of the other teachers is that his tahfiz training has not taken place in a British dar ul-Ulum, like the other teachers at the school.[7] Instead he has attended supplementary Islamic education while also attending a mainstream secular school (i.e., he represents the experiences of moving between secular and Islamic education that is in focus of my project).[8]

Growing up in a "little sleepy town" in northern England, Ibrahim recalls that in his childhood mosques were not really established, that the buildings would be converted churches or houses. Ibrahim went to a state school, but every afternoon between 5 p.m. and 7 p.m. he attended supplementary classes starting when he was around 4 years old continuing until he was 18. In the British context, this kind of daily supplementary education is not at all unusual. Many Muslim families, especially from the Indian subcontinent, attend such classes either on a daily or weekly basis.[9]

Ibrahim says the model used for teaching in supplementary classes when he was a child was "a copy of the Indian Deoband model of education."[10] There was a strong focus on memorization but stories of the prophets, hadiths etc. were also taught:

> Different days had different things. One day was about the tenants of the religion, one day the practices, its called fiq, so it was different subjects, depending on the teacher as well. Memorization was always an integral part. It was memorizing quotes, memorizing Arabic Quran, memorizing hadiths as well, there was always these three.

Even if quotes and hadiths were also memorized, it was the reading, reciting, and memorization of the Quran that was president. This is neither unique for Ibrahim nor for the Deoband model but represent what many Muslims regard as the most important aspect of Islamic education.[11] As we all know, despite what grownups might think is essential to learn, children do not always agree or appreciate their concern: Ibrahim says he used to hate going to the supplementary classes when he was very little, but that after some time, it became like a "social club."

Because the traditional method of teaching the Quran is highly individualized, for each student reading the memorized passage for the teacher at the time, contact time with the teacher was normally not more than 15–20 minutes and the rest could be spent socializing (intended for revising homework though …).

Teaching tahfiz and tajwid

The traditional Quran education, *tahfiz*, is a method that is characterized by memorization, rote learning and person-to-person transmission of knowledge. The art of reciting, *tajwid*, refers to the rules governing pronunciation during recitation and is a highly regarded skill in Muslim societies. According to Kristina Nelson, it is important to understand tajwid because it "preserves the nature of a revelation whose meaning is expressed as much by its sound as by a comprehensive set of regulations which govern many of the parameters of the sound production, such as duration of syllable, vocal timbre and pronunciation."[12]

In many ways Quran education may appear to clash with the ethos, as well as other features, of secular education. In secular schooling, learning is today often described as an open, interactive process in which the student actively constructs knowledge and reaches understanding by questioning and receiving answers from either the teacher or other sources.[13] Dichotomizing these two traditions would thus be to neglect important aspects of teaching and learning that at first sight might seem opposing each other but also to neglect their communalities and complementarity and how individuals like Ibrahim bring forward the benefits of experiencing both. To balance our understanding of his experiences as well as their possible complementarity I would like to start by discussing memorization of the Quran in terms (1) cultural capital and (2) liturgical literacy, but also as (3) a skill that according to Ibrahim, as well as his fellow teachers, can bring value to secular school subjects.

Cultural capital and liturgical literacy

Within Muslim communities the ability to recognize a quotation from the Quran or place Quranic references in appropriate contexts is also seen as a mark of good education.[14] Quranic memorization is also considered important to teach the little child (often like Ibrahim already at 4) because it is understood as "an integral part of learning to be human and Muslim," not a "high tradition" meant for a few chosen people.[15] This brings us to my second point and the concept of cultural capital, that is, those symbolic assets that are prized by several groups within a given society as being more valuable than material assets.[16]

Cultural capital[17] is concept that most often is used for analysis of the mezo-level of society. To bridge the gap to the empirical level of my material I have found the concept of "liturgical literacy" useful.[18] It refers to the practice of using religious texts in liturgy, where understanding of the content is not in focus, but the ability to memorize and use it.

It is a form of literacy that is essential to ritual and devotional practices, a literacy considered necessary for Muslims to have because the Quran is considered a "prayer book, lectionary and hymnal rolled into one." Liturgical literacy has often been ostracized in relation to main stream schooling.[19] Memorizing the Quran is thus not a kind of learning that is limited to mere intellectual involvement with a text, not only the head but also "the heart." Thereby it involves incorporating the "speech of God" into the pupils' being and making it a part of their physical repertoires. In Ibrahim's words

> My own experience is that as soon as you start memorizing the Quran, it has a direct impact on the heart, I am not in control of how I feel, I can feel myself changing, that is how real this Quran is, I have memorized books for university when I was trying to, and my A-levels I was memorizing the Chemistry for the sake, but I forgot it straight away, as soon as the exam finished. This Quran, is strange in the way it, spiritually, I don't know what it is, I don't know what it is. It makes me feel happy!

In this sense it provides an example of how the words of the Quran become embodied.[20] The spiritual dimension of the act of memorizing can hardly be overemphasized because it is the actual speech of God that is said to become embodied through the process of learning the Quran's verses by heart. Ideally embodying the text should also involve acting according to its norms and regulations.[21]

Memorization as a skill

Ibrahim, as well as the other teachers at the school, repeatedly point to benefits and positive connection between hifz as a skill and secular subjects, more often in terms of hifz having a positive effect on secular subject than the opposite: "One big thing that comes through the hifz class as well, is the memorization, capability. They can memorize, their brains, they get into the routine of memorizing and delivering through the hifz they can naturally apply that to, I have noticed."

The teachers thus argue that although memorization as a skill is not as prominent, or brought forward as important (as it used to be) in modern secular education it is still clearly there: For example, when learning a language new words need to be memorized, and in natural sciences and mathematics, certain formulas need to be learned by rote and before exams. But memorization is, according to Ibrahim and his fellow teachers, only one of several beneficial skills that students learn from hifz. They also bring forward skills as confidence, revision and respect for learning, all needed in most forms of education:

> But generally I would say that it is an excellent tool for preparing pupils in terms of focus and in terms of them getting the confidence. When someone realizes that they can look at alien texts and memorize it you know, automatically it gives them that boos and that confidence that I can go into a English and science and maths.

This positive way of viewing memorization stands in stark contrast to the view reflected in majority society. A report from the Institute for Public Policy Research about "'Madrasas' in the British media" reflects that most articles in the media state a negative impact of Quran education in terms of educational outcome.[22] It is perceived as negative because it takes time from homework and other leisure time activities, but also because it is sometimes connected to radicalization.[23]

According to Ibrahim, as well as other teachers, the tafiz training makes up an important reason why parents choose the school, that they have a good reputation for teaching hifz in balance with secular subjects. The hifz-teachers tell me that although they spent their first 3 to 4 years of Islamic education at the Dar ul-Ulum memorizing the Quran and then continued with other Islamic sciences, here at the school they must do it differently. Even if hifz training as such has as its ultimate goal to preserve and transmit the Quran, it is noticeable that when the context changes, so does the teaching.

Becaue Ibrahim's school is a day school, less hours are spent on hifz and the students have many more distractions than at a boarding school (dar ul-ulum). Tafiz thus becomes more of an ordinary school subject than a way of living which it was for those who learned at boarding. It is thus not only the fact that the school is a day school compared to a boarding school that has put pressure on Ibrahim and his fellow teachers to change the way of teaching from more traditional ways. The situation for Muslim schools have also changed dramatically.

Time of turbulence

The past 2 years have been turbulent for Ibrahim as well as other teachers of Muslim schools in East London. Several schools were in 2014 criticized by Ofstead (Office for Standards in Education, i.e., British school inspection) for having a "too narrow" Islamic curriculum and for not actively promoting "British values." Subsequently Muslim schools in East London have also been pictured in the media for posing a "radicalization risk."[24] These inspections, but also downgrading of several Muslim schools, suggests a growing "nervousness" about private Muslim school but also Islam in the United Kingdom.[25]

This situation has led to major changes at the school, a situation that Ibrahim claims, despite the pressures has brought a lot of good: "I think it was a wake up call personally. Wake up the Muslim schools here, stop sleeping, kind of. I don't have the vocabulary for this, sleeping in this very ancient methodology, just teaching pedantic Islam."

The Ofstead inspections should be viewed in the light of the developments in Britain over the past decade: In 2005 the chief inspector of schools expressed concern that Muslim schools were not adequately preparing their pupils for entry into British society.

It was the London bombings (2005) that brought the general question of Islam (and Islamic education) to the forefront of the policy agenda, in addition to such earlier events as 9/11, the Bradford riots (2001), and Britain's involvement in the Afghan (2001) and Iraqi (2003) wars. This troubling chain of events sharply polarized the debate on Muslim education in an environment that had already been fraught with tensions and disagreement. A new discourse on the cultural representation of Muslims emerged, predominantly framed by anxieties fomented by militant extremism. In 2002, citizenship education was introduced in all schools, and in 2007, those schools that were publicly funded but privately run (such as the Muslim schools) were obliged to actively stimulate social cohesion.[26]

In the aftermath of the London bombings, this issue took on a greater mood of urgency and resulted in the inauguration of special programs for the development of citizenship education within several Muslim faith schools. Later research has shown that many Muslim schools use Islam and the Quran to support citizenship education, with students tending to draw on Islamic values when developing a Muslim national identity that promotes solidarity and democratic values.[27]

The fact that some Muslim schools characterize IRE as a type of citizenship education to promote social cohesion can be viewed as an attempt to facilitate Muslim integration and engagement in British society. Although a large amount of research has been conducted on RE in Britain, the number of studies dealing with the content of IRE is still rather small. On top of earlier events, the "Trojan Horse affair" in 2014, where British media leaked an anonymous letter alleging that Salafists were taking over schools in Birmingham to promote their specific agenda, an accusation that in the end proved not to be true, shows that the matter of Islam and education remains a highly contentious issue in British society.[28] Related to this is the issue of Islamophobia, where researchers repeatedly point to its rise in British society.[29]

As a knee-jerk reaction to the Trojan horse affair, but also the so called "prevent strategy"[30] Ofsted's remit has been extended to scrutinize also values. The recent inspections on Muslim schools in East London came as a consequence, and in the Media the schools were bunched together and claimed to teach "too much Islam" and that this could lead to extremism.[31] It needs to be mentioned that Ofsted has been highly criticized for "straying beyond its legal brief."[32]

As already mentioned, Ibrahim views the critique in a positive light. When asked why Ofsted inspections were needed to start the changes he responds:

> East London has developed into … it did not develop. Because of in the 80ies and the 70ies there was a lot of racism they had to really kind of defend _ _ _ they still try to protect themselves from the racism that predominantly was there in the 80ies and early 90ies.

Ibrahim's argument resembles the arguments of educational philosopher Michael Merry who claims that institutional racism is an important aspect of what empirical researchers often avoid when explaining the popularity of religious minority (Muslim) schools in a secular Europe.[33]

The interviews with Ibrahim, as well as his fellow teachers, show that they experienced a gap between hifz and secular education in their own training. To a certain extent they saw this gap as problematic. In the effort of overcoming this gap Ibrahim and his fellow teachers view themselves as "bridge builders" between traditional and modern educational perspectives. The teachers' stories show a variation in terms of favoring the skill of memorization that can be used for "business" to highlighting the more ethical and spiritual aspects. Some favor teaching understanding parallel to memorization, others favor the more classical way of teaching where memorization is seen as a necessary first step before understanding can be start.

For Ibrahim and his colleagues, the Ofsted critique thus led to that they sat down and discussed how they could change, although still keeping their distinguish profile. One decision that was to put further emphasis on "British values"[34] and about other religions:

> I can teach this [British Values], I can teach hadith through this, being a good citizen. Islam tells them to be a good citizen, I can teach them Medina model, so all of this can be applied Islamic. You know, applied Islam instead of just teaching them. It is good for them as well, to be here and learn about these other religions.

One of the reasons why he finds this important is that:

> The kids will identify more. Suburban kids living in London identify more to the diversity which is how religious studies is being taught, with the backbone being Islamic studies. Islam does not have to be so feverently taught you know, this is what the prophet did. I can teach it through Hinduism, I can teach it through Buddhism. There are so many linking morals with all the other religions, that there is no need for me personally to tell them that this religion is the best.

The stance taken in discussions is keeping the tradition of hifz but strengthening other sides, but also to get more cooperative and creative learning on the schedule. Ibrahim draws on his own trajectory of hifz when arguing for changes, remembering teachers from his own supplementary education that really sparked his interest.

> Sometimes the teacher would be replaced and you get a really young teacher, like starting his career. He will sit down and make it fun. Colorful and you would memorize it. I remember my early days, the best teachers, were the ones who would make us memorize sayings but there was always a story behind it, like a moral, you know you have Aesop fables. He would relate the stories behind the prophet.

According to Ibrahim, what can thus really make a difference is this more interactive style of teaching where teachers explain more about the meaning: "There is geography inside, there is history inside, you know, it won't be British history, but there is a lot of historical psychology inside, you will see the thirst for power, the thirst for conquering other people taking over their lands, its there mentioned in the Quran."

Ibrahim tells also teach world religions through this method:

> For example Buddhism, the enlightenment, you make the link to the prophet (*sallā llāhu 'alay-hi wa-sallam*), he was enlightened and then we talk a little bit so that they can see the links. Because a lot of these kids are coming in here with a very polarized idea that we are right and everybody else is wrong. Yes, I need to get rid of that. It is not part of Islam.

Ibrahim's own teaching about world religions is most clearly affected by his own knowledge of hifz. He says he often brings out passages from the Quran, but also hadith to support his arguments along the lines represented by the quotes above. He is also one of the teachers who has argued for bringing hifz closer to other school subject. He claims that one of the reasons why he feels strongly for this is because of his own secular studies of Arabic at the university: "I was learning Arabic from non-Muslims and started to under-stand the Quran." After not practicing Islam in his late teens secular studies at the university made him a practicing Muslim again saying "You know I think I personally learned most of my Islam at university". He recalls the situation:

> People around me are asking questions, because university is all about asking questions. And my experience, I went to Glastonbury festival, one of my very close friends Alice, she is a devout, she worships the sun, the moon, like that, she is still a very close friend of mine, all these differences. All of this is making me understanding.

It was also at university where he completed his hifz training, an experience that has had crucial impact on him and his life:

> I was like my first year university: September, October, November, December. I remember the Christmas parties, everybody was like come on, and I was: "no no I need to finish my hifz man." This is a spiritual time for me, I cannot go to all of these parties, and they used to go to these parties, and I am there trying to memorize the Quran and they coming back two or three o' clock half-drunk,

someone is playing the saxophone, smoke cannabis. I don't know what is happening, but they all used to come to my room and they used to love listening to me, reciting the Quran. And I used to make them pot-noodles, cause they were all hungry sometimes. I used to boil the kettle and bring the noodle, and they used to sit and become sober and they used to say, I remember M: "I don't know what you are saying but we know you are chanting this 14th century Arabic, but it is beautiful." And I just used to be reciting. And then I finished it in January, the 4th I think. I finally finished my final verses of the Quran and I remember dreams on everything became so clear. I was no longer making decisions by myself, but I was basically being led by another force I cannot put my finger on what it was, the only explanation that I can see is that I can feel that it is a God out there. That's Allah, and he is not letting me make silly decisions, like I used to before.

Ibrahim's own experience of hifz and university studies has been crucial for his way of teaching and thinking about education. He wants the students to see the benefits of interacting with people from other religions, in a similar way as he did and bring forward the value of hifz for the the students' "hearts and love of God." Some parents have been critical becaue they want more "madrasa-style" teaching, but "every time the parents come to me, they understand the perspective, and they never complain after that." He says that it has happened that parents do not want them to take their children to church visits: "But you can learn about a church" and "we respect parents who do not want them to visit church, they do not have to, we are not going to force them, but slowly, slowly it will open up their minds."

Continuity and change

The preservation and teaching of Islam is understandably of utter importance for Ibrahim and his colleagues. Although the goal of hifz is the transmission and protection of the Quran, and has its very specific history and methods, it is obvious that this educational process is not possible to withdraw from context. Ibrahim's experience of moving between Islamic and secular education, but also teaching at the school, puts the dichotomy between secular and Islamic education into question. It makes clear that, according to his perspective, these two educations have been beneficial to each other.

Ibrahim's and the other teachers' perspective on the benefits of hifz in relation to other school subjects stands in contrast to how memorization of the Quran is viewed by majority society. A question that arises from this dichotomous situation is if what can be understood as a capital in the Muslim context risks turning into a cost when brought outside the Muslim context, although there seem to be many benefits of instead viewing them as supplementary to each other.

His educational trajectory also brings forward the reasons why it is important and interesting to study religious education. In any context, the concern with teaching and defining religious knowledge, beliefs, values, and skills to the young can be understood as the jugular vein[35] of a religious tradition. Without some kind of teaching, a religious tradition simply cannot continue. For a majority religion, the society in itself communicates the tradition through national history and school system. Sometimes in an open and explicit sense, but sometimes in more subtle ways.[36] For a minority, investment in teaching in the formal institutions of a modern nation-state's education system is a powerful and historically specific civic expression of the right to existence but also to belong. The realities help to explain why schooling is so often a point of social struggle and contestation. The content of what is taught speaks to future ideals.

Funding

Funding was received from Marie Sklodowska Curie Actions FP7.

Notes

1. Jill Lepore, "Love Too Much; Reflections on Microhisotry and Biography," *The Journal of American History* 88, no. 1 (2001): 129–44.
2. A person who has memorized the Quran is called *hafiz*. Memorization of the Quran is often referred to as the back bone of Islamic education stems from the Quran viewed as the revealed word of God, and thus a type of miracle; Ahmad Von Denffer, *Ulum al-Qur'an: An introduction to the Sciences of the Qur'an* (Leicestershire, UK: The Islamic Foundation, 2003).
3. For previous research on young Muslims in East London see, for example, Daniel DeHanas, "Elastic Ortodoxy: The Tactics of Young Muslim Identity in the East End of London," In *Everyday Lived Islam in Europe* (Farnham, UK: Ashgate, 2013), 69–84.
4. The paper is based on semi-structured interviews conducted October 6–7, 2015 and February 11, 2016, the interviews are part of the larger project mentioned in the introduction.
5. Oliver Leaman (Ed.), *The Qu'ran, An Encyclopedia* (Milton Park, UK: Routledge, 2006). The word Quran or al-Quran means "the recitation," both in the sense of performance and in the sense of instruction; William A. Graham, *Beyond the Written Word: Oral Aspects of Scripture in the History of Religion* (Cambridge, UK: Cambridge University Press, 1987); Michael Anthony Sells, *Approaching the Quran: The Early Revelations* (Ashland, OR: White Cloud Press, 1999; Von Denffer 2003, 17). As such, the recitation of the Quran is viewed not only as an act of memorization and oral performance, but also as an act of "worship, meditation and sublime aesthetic enjoyment" (Denny Mathewson, 1995, 397). In the early history of Islam, it was the recitation of the Quran that was thought to protect it from alteration.
6. Note that live recitation is often considered more complete than the written text because it contains the rhythms and sounds of the words. See, for example, Safwat M. Halilovic, 2005, *Hifz Memorization of the Qur'an* (Von Denffer, 2003, 166); or Marwan Ibrahim Al-Kaysi, *Morals and Manners in Islam: A Guide to Islamic Adab* (Leicester, UK: Islamic Foundation, 1986), see 103–4 for examples of instructions in the recitation of the Quran.
7. The teachers who teach hifz are also hafiz, but all are trained at a specific British dar-ul Ulum, a private Islamic boarding school that they attended from the age of 10–11 to 19–20.

8. The project is called "Experiences of Islamic and Secular Education in Sweden and Britain" (http://www.sh.se/p3/ext/content.nsf/aget?openagent&key=projekt_page_eng_1415628308602) and is funded by Funded by Swedish Research Council and Marie Sklodowska Curie Actions.

9. Karamat Iqbal, 2016, PhD dissertation from University of Warwick.

10. See, for example, Ebrahim Moosa, *What is a Madrasa?* (Chapel Hill, NC: University of North Carolina Press, 2015) and Kristina Nelson, *The Art of Reciting the Qur'an* (Cairo, Egypt: American University in Cairo Press, 2001) about the Deoband model of Islamic education.

11. Jonathan Berkey, *The Transmission of Knowledge in Medieval Cairo: A Social History of Islamic Education* (Princeton, NJ: Princeton University Press, 1992); Von Denffer 2003. Graham (1987, 61) wrote "the learning of at least some part of the divine word by heart is the single most common early learning experience shared in some degree by all Muslims." See also Sebastian Günther, "The 9th Century Muslim Scholars Ibn Saphun and al-Jahiz on Pedagogy and Didactics," in *Ideas, Images, and Methods of Portrayal: Insights Onto Classical Arabic Literature and Civilization*, edited by Sebastian Günther (Leiden, The Netherands: Brill, 2005), 89–128. Regarding the views of two 9th century scholars on the teaching of the Quran.

12. Nelson, 2001, 14.

13. Helene N. Boyle, "Memorization and Learning in Islamic Schools," In *Islam and Education Myths and Truths,* edited by Wadad Kadi and Victor Billeh (Chicago, IL: The University of Chicago Press), 172–189; Bill Gent, "The Hidden Olympians: The role of huffaz, in the Englsih Muslim community," *Contemporary Islam* 10 (2016): 17–34.

14. Mustansir Mir, "The Quran in Muslim Thought and Practice," In *The Oxford Encyclopedia of the Modern Islamic World*, edited by John L. Esposito (New York, NY: Oxford University Press, 1994), 394–96. See also, for example, Daniel A. Wagner, and Abdelhamid Loft, "Traditional Islamic Education in Marocco: Sociohistorical and Psychological Perspectives," *Comparative Education Review* 24, no. 2 (1980): 238–51.

15. Dale F. Eickelman, *Knowledge and Power in Morocco: The Education of a Twentieth-Century Notable* (Princeton, NJ: Princeton University Press, 1985). For an updated version, see Dale F. Eickelman, "Madrasas in Morocco: Their Vanishing Public Role," In *Schooling Islam: The Culture and Politics of Modern Muslim Education*, edited by Muhammad Qasim Zaman and Robert W. Hefner (Princeton, NJ: Princeton University Press, 2007), 131–48. See also Von Denffer, 2003, 174, who provides the following list of reasons for memorising the Quran: It was the sunna of the Prophet; it is required for prayer; it is useful for *dawa;* it leads to more remembrance of God as well as to determination; it leads to deeper faith and understanding.

16. Pierre Bourdieu, *The State Nobility: Elite Schools in the Field of Power* (Lauretta C. Clough, Trans.), (Stanford, CA: Stanford University Press, 1996).

17. "Cultural capital" can be described as those symbolic assets that are praised by several groups within a given society as being more valuable than material assets.

18. Rosowsky, Andrey, *Heavenly Readings Liturgical Literacy in a Multilingual Context* (Bristol, UK: Multilingual Matters, 2008).

19. Rosowsky, 2008, 15.

20. According to Ross, 2004, 170, all learning involves the body, and embodied learning is a fundamental part of selfhood and cultural belonging. Ross, Janice, "The Instructable Body: Student Bodies from Classrooms to Prisons," In *Knowing Bodies, Moving Minds: Towards Embodied Teaching and Learning,* edited by Liora Bresler (Dordrecht, The Netherlandse: Kluwer Academic, 2004), 169–81.

21. Halilovic 2005.

22. Cherti Maryam, Alex Glennie, and Laura Bradley, *Madrasas in the British Media* (London, UK: Institute for Public Policy Research, 2011). This report reflects that most articles state a negative impact in terms of educational outcome, claiming that pressures from madrasas draw attention from mainstream school subjects.

23. See references to the media in Cherti, 2011.

24. Richard Adams and Aisha Gani, "'Radicalisation risk' at six Muslim schools in London," *The Guardian*, November 21, 2014. http://www.theguardian.com/education/2014/nov/21/ofsted-muslim-schools-london-closure-threat

25. Britain's integration policy is historically based on valuing and promoting cultural diversity and multiculturalism. Over the last decade, however, the discourse on multiculturalism appears to have become more negative and intertwined with the political identity of Muslims in particular Meer and Modood, 2014, 666 (Nasar Meer and Tariq Modood, "Cosmopoitanism and integration: is British multiculturalism a 'Zombie category'?," *Identities: Global Studies in Culture and Power* 21, no. 6 (2014): 658–678.). See also Jenny Berglund, *Publicly Funded Islamic Education in Europe and the United States* (Washington, DC: The Brookings Institution, 2015).

26. "Education and Inspections Act 2006," *The National Archives*, http://www.legislation.gov.uk/ukpga/2006/40/contents; see also Panjwani, Farid, "Religion, Citizenship and Hope: Civic Virtues and Education about Muslim Traditions," In *Sage Handbook of Education for Citizenship and Democracy*, edited by James Arthur, Ian Davies, and Carol Hahn (London: Sage Publications, 2008), 292–304, for a discussion on Islam and citizenship education.

27. Peter Mandaville, "Islamic Education in Britain: Approaches to Religious Knowledge," In *Schooling Islam: The Culture and Politics of Modern Muslim Education*, edited by Robert W. Hefner and Muhammad Qasim Zaman (Princeton, NJ: Princeton Univeristy Press, 2007), 224–41. See also Christopher Bagley and Nader Al-Refai, "Citizenship Education: A Study of Muslim Students in Ten Islamic and State Secondary Schools in Britain" In *Reforms in Islamic Education*, edited by Charlene Tan (London, UK: Bloomsbury, 2014), 195–210.

28. The "Trojan Horse Affair" involved secular schools but has, as we will see, still affected attitudes towards private Muslim schools. In March 2014, the British media leaked an anonymous letter alleging that Salafists were taking over schools in Birmingham to promote their specific agenda. Ofsted decided to investigate the matter, as did the Department of Education. They appointed Peter Clarke, a former senior counter-terrorism official to lead its investigation. His report claimed to have found "a coordinated agenda to impose hardline Sunni Islam," following which the Birmingham City Council appointed Ian Kershew to conduct a further investigation. Kershew, however, found "no evidence of a conspiracy," no evidence of violent extremism and no evidence of radicalization or some sort of anti-British agenda; he merely found a desire to improve educational attainments by promoting certain Islamic principles and values. He did warn of governance problems in some of Birmingham's Muslim schools and criticized the city council's role in sanctioning or ignoring such practices. See Robert Jackson, "Inclusive Study of Religions and Non-religious World Views in State- funded Schools: Signposts from the Council of Europe," in *Journal of Social Inclusion* (2016) about the UK "prevent strategy."

29. Chris Allen, *Islamophobia* (London, UK: Ashgate, 2010). See also Runnymede Trust, *Islamophobia: A Challenge to Us All* (Manchester, UK: The Runnymede Trust, 1997), http://www.runnymedetrust.org/publications/17/32.html.

30. Robert Jackson, "Inclusive Study of Religions and Non-religious World Views in State-funded Schools: Signposts from the Council of Europe," *Social Inclusion* 4, no. 2 (2016).

31. See http://www.theguardian.com/education/2014/nov/21/ofsted-muslim-schools-london-closure-threat.

32. See https://news.tes.co.uk/b/opinion/2014/12/10/ofsted-s-chief-inspector-is-not-in-a-position-to-play-god-not-his-subordinate-angels-on-their-visits-to-schools.aspx.

33. Michael Merry, "The Conundrum of Religious Schools in Twenty-first Century Europe," *Comparative Education* 55, no. 1 (2015): 133–56.

34. The concept "British values" has found its way from the British Government's 2011 development of the 'Prevent' strategy to the Counter-Terrorism and Security Act (2015). The introduction of Part 5 of this Act gives the Prevent strategy legal status in schools and colleges in England and Wales. What is typically "British" about them is unclear, instead they represent values that can be found in many liberal societies: "Democracy, the rule of law, individual liberty, and mutual respect and tolerance of those with different faiths and beliefs" (Jackson 2016).

35. "And indeed We have created man, and We know whatever thoughts his inner self develops, and We are closer to him than (his) jugular vein" (Quran 50:16).

36. Jenny Berglund, "Swedish Religion Education: Objective But Marinated in Lutheran Protestantism?" in *Temenos* 49, no. 2 (2013): 165–84.

Islamic Modernism and Colonial Education in Northern Nigeria: Na'ibi Sulaiman Wali (1927–2013)

Alexander Thurston

ABSTRACT

From the colonial period on, elite education in northern Nigeria has been an arena marked by ambivalence over how to combine Islam with "modernity"—a concept with as many different definitions as the protagonists involved in the debate. In postcolonial northern Nigeria, graduates of elite schools often evinced discomfort with their own education. This discomfort was visible in the generation of northern Muslim elites who were trained in colonial schools but whose careers peaked after independence. To explore the interrelationships among education, Islam, and modernism, this article discusses the life of Na'ibi Sulaiman Wali (1927–2013).

In the twentieth century, northern Nigeria experienced tremendous social and political change, transforming the public role of Islam in this Muslim-majority region and bringing visibility to new classes of religious intellectuals and activists. Education featured in this process as both an instrument and a symbol of change. Struggles over the character and trajectory of mass education in northern Nigeria have been heated;[1] fierce debates have also surrounded elite education, the topic of this article.

From the colonial period on, elite education in northern Nigeria has been an arena marked by profound ambivalence over how to combine Islam with "modernity"—a concept with as many different definitions as the protagonists involved in the debate. Strikingly, in northern Nigeria it has been the graduates of elite schools who have often evinced the greatest discomfort with their education. This discomfort was particularly visible in the generation of northern Muslim elites who were trained in colonial schools but whose careers peaked after independence.

Their discomfort gives insights into how various Islamic modernisms were constructed in Nigeria during decolonization. *Islamic modernism*, in Nigeria and around the world, refers to a cluster of Muslim-led movements that concentrated on revitalizing Islam to meet the perceived challenges of European political, economic, military, and scientific dominance, while simultaneously Islamizing European-style "modernity." Such movements often had limited popular appeal, but in Northern Nigeria they were a key feature of elite discourses from the 1940s on.

To explore the interrelationships among elite education, Islam, and modernism, this article discusses the life trajectory of Shaykh Na'ibi Sulaiman Wali (1927–2013). Born near the midpoint of British colonialism in Northern Nigeria (1900–1960), Wali exemplifies hybridity: He hailed from a prominent family within the North's hereditary Muslim ruling elite, but he became a partial critic of that system. His father was a well-regarded Sufi shaykh and teacher in the classical mode of Islamic pedagogy in the region. But the elder Wali also became the headmaster of a British colonial school, reflecting the transformations that colonialism brought even for certain adult Muslims. The younger Wali, for his part, attended the foremost British colonial schools for training Muslim judges and Arabists. His schooling included both a structured sojourn in another decolonizing British territory, Sudan, and a postcolonial study tour in Denmark, focusing on agriculture.

Wali's varied career reflected the breadth of his education: publisher, judge, imam, and advisor to several governments. Wali's writings reflect broader trends among Northern Nigerian Muslim intellectuals of his generation: in the 1950s, this cohort emphasized an effort to make generic Islamic knowledge widely available to the literate Northern public. It was only in the late 1960s and 1970s that this cohort turned to explicitly anticolonial and Islamic modernist writing.

Arguments and sources

This article argues that Wali, along with several of his contemporaries who flourished in northern Nigeria between the 1950s and the 1970s, articulated modernist Islamic discourses long after the main wave of global Islamic modernism had supposedly peaked. That northern Nigerian Islamism modernism flourished later than, for example, Egyptian Islamic modernism, reflects the different paths of colonial encounters in those countries, especially the different trajectories of colonial education.

Wali's brand of Islamic modernism was both a product of and a reaction to the British colonial modernization effort. This modernism took as its targets "traditional" Islamic thought on the one hand, and colonialism and "neo-colonialism" on the other. A strategy of rhetorical triangulation helped Islamic modernists to distance themselves from both traditionalism and colonialism, even as they continued to carry forward some elements of both those forces.

The article draws on diverse sources, especially Wali's two major polemical tracts, *Duniya, Ina Za Ki da Mu?* (World, Where Are You Taking Us?, 1974) and *Mu Koma Kan Hanya* (Let Us Get Back on the Path, 1975). In these texts, Wali articulated his brand of Islamic modernism and anti-colonialism. The article contextualizes these sources by examining the history of politics, Muslim activism, and publishing in Northern Nigeria in the late colonial and early independence periods.

These sources and contexts help to situate Wali and his peers as "Muslim activist intellectuals," part of a global contingent of thinkers who participated in core debates that occurred throughout the Muslim world during the twentieth century.[2] These debates, both for Islamic modernists and other types of Muslim activists, centered on several questions: What did it mean to be truly free of European domination? What form should public morality take in newly independent Muslim states? How should Muslim societies balance continuity and renewal? The article's key contribution lies in showing that for Wali and for Northern Nigeria, such debates were not mere reflections of Islamic modernist movements elsewhere, but were anchored in specifically local trajectories of education and politics.

Islamic modernisms: Questions of definition and periodization

Constructing an objective definition of modernity is a fraught exercise, as is the effort to objectively determine whether different actors were modern or not. The concept of modernity is inherently dynamic and perhaps inherently plural as well, making its meaning hard to pin down.[3] To explore how various actors have conceived of "modernity," however, can shed light on the contours of intellectual, social, and political—as well as religious—change. This article eschews objective definitions of modernity in favor of analyzing the subjective definitions used by British colonial administrators and Nigerian Muslim intellectuals.

What this article calls modernism, then, refers to various projects that sought to define, create, and/or appropriate modernity. British colonial modernism, from India to Egypt to Nigeria, revolved around the combination of technological spectacle (such as massive railroads[4] and dams[5]) with a project of guided social change for colonized peoples. British officials' feelings about directing social change, however, were characterized by recurring anxieties, particularly when it came to elite education. British planners feared that elite colonial schools would produce graduates who were simultaneously alienated from their original communities and unassimilable into European modernity. In colonial Northern Nigeria, British schools aimed to produce Muslim elites who were open to gradual social change but who remained politically quiescent and culturally "authentic"—at least in terms of what the British considered proper politics and authentic culture.

Islamic modernism also represented a dual effort: "the self-conscious adoption of 'modern' values" and "the usage of a self-consciously Islamic discourse."[6] Much scholarship on Islamic modernism has focused on the intellectual triumvirate of the globe-trotting Jamal al-Din al-Afghani (1838–1897), the Egyptian Muhammad 'Abduh (1849–1905), and the Syria-born

Muhammad Rashid Rida (1865–1935), as well as their intellectual antecedents, such as the Egyptian Rifa'a al-Tahtawi (1801–1873).[7]

Such scholarship has generated two problems. First, Islamic modernism is often depicted as a singular phenomenon. This depiction creates the impression that where Islamic modernism existed, it emerged out of a singular intellectual network with figures like 'Abduh at its center. In colonial Northern Nigeria, Islamic modernist discourses appeared from the ground up – that is, among graduates of colonial schools who likely had never read al-Afghani, 'Abduh, or Rida, at least as students and young professionals, but who reached similar conclusions on their own.

Second, Islamic modernism is often depicted as a phenomenon with a particular lifespan: 1840–1940, in one influential account.[8] Such periodizations have contributed to linear and teleological readings of nineteenth- and twentieth-century history in the Arab and Muslim worlds. For example, Ibrahim Abu-Rabi' writes, "Three main concepts can sum up the progression of Arab thought from the early nineteenth century to the present: (1) *nahḍah* (renaissance), (2) *thawrah* (revolution), and (3) *'awdah* (return to the foundations."[9] Abu-Rabi's three concepts refer respectively to the Islamic modernism associated with 'Abduh, the revolution associated with the Free Officers in Egypt, and the so-called wave of "Islamic fundamentalism" and "Islamism" after 1967. This linear depiction of Arab thought, which takes Egypt as its central example, is often generalized to the entire Muslim world.

In late colonial and early independent Northern Nigeria, elite intellectuals and their political allies were experimenting with Islamic modernism long after 1940. Islamic modernism in Northern Nigeria arose out of largely local encounters, especially the encounter of British colonial educational policies with the Muslim elites who graduated from British-run schools. Islamic modernism in Northern Nigeria followed its own trajectory, one that does not correspond to that of Islamic modernism in the Arab world.

Tracing the multiple trajectories of Islamic modernism in the world after World War II expands understanding of the twentieth century as a period of persistent experimentation regarding Islam and public life. This perspective also refocuses attention on the importance of the colonial encounter and decolonization for contributing to the forms that experimentation took in different societies. Not all colonial encounters fit one mold, and consequently decolonization took different trajectories and so did constructions of secularism and/or public Islam. In Northern Nigeria, British colonial policymakers explicitly positioned many of their policies as reactions to or departures from previous policies elsewhere, especially India and Egypt, or as sequels to and modifications of policies in Sudan.

For Islamic modernism, this means that conditions for thinkers like Na'ibi Sulaiman Wali in Northern Nigeria were fundamentally different from the conditions faced by thinkers like Muhammad 'Abduh in Egypt. Exposure to pan-Islamic influences was lower in colonial Northern Nigeria, because colonial authorities worked hard to restrict Northern Muslims' contact with the broader Muslim world. There was no equivalent to Jamal al-Din al-Afghani in Northern Nigeria—no wandering pan-Islamic thinker, in close dialogue and debate with thinkers in Europe, who had the ear of rulers—until at least the 1940s. Egypt and Northern Nigeria, in other words, followed fundamentally different timelines.

On one level, Northern Nigeria could be seen as lagging behind Egypt by four or five decades. But context matters. When Islamic modernism emerged in Egypt, Syria, and elsewhere in the late nineteenth and early twentieth centuries, it had a major intellectual impact but faced profound institutional resistance—'Abduh's proposed reforms of al-Azhar University were in the end appropriated, modified, and managed by conservatives,[10] whereas modernists in Damascus found that "their marginal social position restricted the effect of their arguments."[11] This does not mean that Islamic modernism in the Middle East came to naught: The early twentieth-century Islamic modernism of Egypt, Syria, and elsewhere had important echoes in the political and societal program of the Muslim Brotherhood and even, obliquely, in what has come to be known as the Salafi movement or "approach" (*manhaj*). Yet in its own time, the Egyptian and Syrian Islamic modernism had limited institutional success.

In contrast, the Islamic modernism of Northern Nigeria, especially in the 1950s and 1960s, became the dominant ideology of the ruling Muslim elite. The Premier of the Northern Region from 1954 to 1966, Ahmadu Bello (1910–1966), interwove Islamic modernism with campaigns to spread Islam, reinvent and revitalize the North's Islamic heritage, and unify the North's different Muslim communities under the banner of a Sufi-inspired charismatic community.

Wali was a key participant in these ideological endeavors. He served as the Secretary to the Northern Government from 1960 to 1968 and was one of the founders of Bello's Jama'at Nasr al-Islam (Society for the Victory of Islam), an organization that attempted to provide religious unity to Northern Muslims. Before examining Wali's life, however, it is worthwhile to describe the emergence of Islamic modernism in colonial Northern Nigeria.

The roots of Islamic modernism in colonial Northern Nigeria

Anticolonial thought and action, one component of Islamic modernism, circulated in Northern Nigeria from the beginning of the British occupation. As Muhammad Sani Umar has shown, Northern Nigerian Muslims responded to colonial rule in diverse and complex ways that were influenced by the professional, intellectual, and social niches they occupied. One antecedent of the modernist intellectuals was the ulama, who had greater freedom of political movement than the emirs. Umar wrote, "As a class that stood largely outside the colonial administration, the ulama could openly express their views on colonialism without the risk of dismissal that the emirs could not simply ignore."[12] Yet Umar also noted that ulama who served in the administration, such as the Wazir Junaidu (d. 1997), often felt it necessary to tone down their opposition to certain colonial policies and to make "muted complaints against the moral and religious decline that the ulama saw resulting from colonialism."[13] This idea of moral decline would also come to characterize the construction of history that anticolonial modernists set forth; the modernists would lament the passing of an age of higher moral character while simultaneously attacking tradition and advocating their brand of progress.

If the ulama in general were one source of anticolonial thought, the Northern Provinces Law School (NPLS; discussed further below), the British colonial administration's hub for training "modernized" ulama and a key step in Wali's educational trajectory, was a fount of indigenous modernism. Forms of Islamic modernism were on display at NPLS by the early 1940s. In 1943, a scholar gave a speech at NPLS using core themes of Islamic modernism: He decried an alleged lack of "progress" in Muslim countries and attacked the form of asceticism that renounced worldly achievement and technological gain. An excerpt follows,

> He errs who thinks that this world was created only for the kafir (unbeliever) … and [thinks] that he whose clothes are dirty, and whose food disgusting, is the one who has arrived at the reality of piety … This kind of thinking has set Muslims back. Instead of them being progressives they have ended up on their beds sleeping."[14]

The speaker's core themes and metaphors—the idea that Muslims were asleep, and that they should seek both worldly progress and salvation in the afterlife—would reappear in texts like Wali's *Mu Koma kan Hanya*.

Another source of Northern Nigerian Islamic modernism in the late colonial period was an emerging class of anticolonial intellectuals, political leaders, and literary figures, such as Aminu Kano (1920–1983) and Sa'adu Zungur (1915–1958). Many of the Arabophone elites who graduated from NPLS were affiliated with the Northern People's Congress (NPC), the dominant political party of independence-era Northern Nigeria, and not with Kano's Northern Elements Progressive Union (NEPU), a leftist opposition party. But the Arabophones and NEPU's intellectuals shared common ideals when it came to "modernizing" reforms such as founding Islamiyya schools (hybrid schools where Western sciences were taught alongside Islamic ones) and advancing the status of women.

Zungur was a particular inspiration to his younger contemporaries, including Wali. Zungur's educational path partly overlapped with theirs, though Zungur and Aminu Kano received an Anglophone rather than an Arabophone colonial education. Zungur was given a traditional Islamic education by his father, but also attended Bauchi Provincial Primary School (1920–1926) and Katsina College (1929–1934). In 1934, he became "the first Northern Nigerian to be sponsored by the colonial administration for advanced studies outside the North" and attended Yaba Higher College in Lagos for at least one term.[15] Zungur found coursework at Yaba simplistic but was influenced by his time in Lagos, where he participated in nationalist organizations. From 1935 to 1943, Zungur worked in the colonial Health Department, first in Kano and, after 1939, in Zaria. He wrote poetry and worked to promote civic associations, founding a short-lived branch of the Egyptian Young Men's Muslim Association in Kano and establishing a Hausa Youths Keep Fit Class in Zaria.

Zungur's writings exhibited the antitraditionalism that would characterize other modernists' work. In a series of editorials in *Gaskiya Ta Fi Kwabo* in 1942–1943, he alleged that certain practices—"offering to the dead, transvestism and the practice of wake-weeping by widows on the night of their third day of mourning"—were un-Islamic.[16] Amid the resulting controversy, Zungur was dismissed from colonial service in 1943 and returned to his native Bauchi. There he became a core member of another civic association, the Bauchi Discussion Circle, formed in 1943 with representation from the aristocracy, the Native Authority, and young educated Northern Nigerians such as Aminu Kano and Abubakar Tafawa Balewa (1912–1966, who later served as Nigeria's first Prime Minister).[17] The Circle debated religious issues but also discussed scientific and professional concerns. From the mid-1940s on, Zungur was involved in several political parties, including the NCNC and the NPC, before finding a home, after approximately 1952, in NEPU. After years of ill health, he died in 1958.

Northern Islamic modernists saw in Zungur a pioneer and a voice that time had vindicated. One modernist wrote that Zungur "was one of the extraordinary Nigerians who combined Arabic and English culture. He was a literary man and a politician faithful to his country, and an enemy of the first class to the odious colonialist."[18] Wali was even more effusive in his praise: "This Shaykh called out warnings and advice to the other brothers but it was not heeded!"[19] After quoting a poem of Zungur's on the North's moral decay, where Zungur complains of prostitutes, beggars, and beer halls, Wali wrote, "All those diseases that the late [Mallam] Sa'adu Zungur mentioned, all are out in the open, and we are certain that they are among the major things that have violated our humanity, destroyed our system and made our country relinquish the benefit that modernity has brought!"[20] Zungur's modernism, in later modernists' reading, had identified negative aspects of both tradition and colonial modernity, and had pointed a way toward intellectual and moral renewal on Islamic terms.

The shifting vantage point of postcoloniality altered the reception of Zungur's work over time. Professor Dandatti Abdulkadir, another member of the Northern scholarly elite of this generation, wrote in his 1974 *The*

Poetry, Life, and Opinions of Sa'adu Zungur that the poet's writings took on particular significance after the collapse of Nigeria's First Republic in a 1966 coup. Abdulkadir wrote that Zungur's poem *Arewa Jumhuriya Ko Mulukiya* (Hausa: "The North, a Republic or a Monarchy?"), in which he argued for a monarchy in Northern Nigeria and warned of conflict with the South in the event of republican rule, "had not been given much importance until after the beginning of the recent Nigerian crisis. Now people realise that Sa'adu has a message to impart—a message that has turned out to be a prophecy."[21]

Zungur's *Arewa* is notable for how it looks both backward, to the perceived religious golden age of northern Nigeria's pre-colonial jihad period—

> Truly Shehu Abdullahi [dan Fodio, a pre-colonial Muslim scholar and key jihad leader] left us an inheritance of truth/Of learning, of wisdom, of religion—all— and of skill in managing worldly matters./But we have degenerated, we have scattered it to the winds, see how today we are a laughing stock!/Birds and trap —both gone! By Allah, we have thrown away the world!/Ignorance has made us spineless, has chained us even to our necks/Has put handcuffs on our wrists, and tied our feet with cord that bites./It has put muzzles on our mouths – instead of eloquence, lies![22]

—and forward, to the need for moral and intellectual renewal in the North:

> As for us, knowledge is what we seek, whether in London or Arabia[23] ... It is our hope is that the entire North will awake to a full knowledge of the world's ways[24]/ ... In sha Allah! Let us cleanse ourselves, in the hope that we may follow what is true./For if the North is full of dissension and wickedness, we lose our defence.[25]

Lines from this poem that expand on the alleged moral decline in the North are excerpted in Wali's *Mu Koma*. Zungur's construction of history—a glorious past, a morally corrupted present, and the acquisition of both technical and religious knowledge (from "London or Arabia") as the key to future renewal—furnished an important heritage for Nigerian Islamic modernists in the early postcolonial period.

Na'ibi Sulaiman Wali: Biographical sketch

Na'ibi Sulaiman Wali was born in 1927 in Kano.[26] His father, Sulaiman Wali (d. 1939), was a classical Muslim scholar and a member of the hereditary Muslim ruling class—in the last year or so of his life, he served as the Wali (counselor) to the Emir of Kano.

As a child and young man, the younger Wali attended a series of colonially administered schools in Kano. These schools were intended to train Muslim judges, teachers of Arabic, and other functionaries whose roles involved working with Islam (court scribes, assistants to Muslim hereditary rulers, etc.).

Wali went to the Elementary School in Kano from 1936 to 1940, then to Shahuci Judicial School from 1942 to 1945, and finally to the NPLS (later renamed the School for Arabic Studies or SAS) from 1945 to 1949.[27]

The trajectory of these schools highlights the complex interactions that occurred in the 1920s and after, involving colonialism, the hereditary Muslim establishment, and the classical system of Islamic education in the region. Shahuci, founded in 1928 in Kano, emerged out of colonial authorities' suggestion to the Emir Abdullahi Bayero (1881–1953) that he move his "Palace Legal Training Unit" out of the palace and formalize it as a training institution for jurists. The emir selected Na'ibi Sulaiman's father, the future Wali Sulaiman, to become the school's first headmaster and teacher. To a small group of students, "handpicked from royal children and their subordinates,"[28] Sulaiman taught a curriculum based in the Maliki legal school of Sunni Islam that featured works such as *Al-Risāla* (Epistle) of Tunisian jurist Ibn Abī Zayd al-Qayrawānī (922–96) and *Tuḥfat al-Ḥukkām* (The Gift of Judges) of Ibn 'Asīm (d. 1426), as well as a secular curriculum that included mathematics, English and Hausa.[29]

At Shahuci and the Law School, pedagogical methods drawn from traditional Islamic schooling in Northern Nigeria—recitation by students followed by commentary from the teacher—were fitted into a regimented framework involving strict timetables, regular examinations, and pedagogical innovations student dramatizations of legal questions. Classical Islamic texts were used to communicate broader themes and encourage understanding of the abstract principles behind religious requirements. A syllabus from the late 1940s at NPLS (by then SAS) said that in the eighth year, instructors teaching eighth year students should "talk to them about justice, consultation, economy and harm of prostitution, drinking wine and gambling."[30]

The schools placed a premium on fostering debate among teachers and students about legal methodology, as well as fostering critical discussion of the spirit of the law. NPLS was run by a combination of British and Sudanese administrators. The Sudanese were imported by the British out of concerns that Northern Nigeria's own Muslim scholars were too conservative and inflexible. With Sudanese scholars, the British felt, the colonial administration could replicate in Northern Nigeria the perceived success of "modernized" schools in Sudan such as Gordon Memorial College. This "modernization" had the result that—rightly or wrongly—the graduates of NPLS sometimes felt that they were better equipped, linguistically and intellectually, than older scholars who had been trained strictly in the classical system. One graduate later recalled:

> I did not welcome to study with the leading scholars around, because I had now become used to an approach quite different from theirs. Most of my former teachers had background in both the European and traditional Islamic schools and that made them to be different ... The city scholars had a less flexible background.[31]

A core component of Islamic modernism in Northern Nigeria, then, was that the graduates of colonial schools began to differentiate themselves from classical scholars. This effort involved the "reproduction" of colonial discourses about modernity,[32] but this effort also featured an implicit anti-colonialism that became more visible as the years wore on.

At Shahuci and NPLS, Wali came to know the men who would become some of Northern Nigeria's foremost Muslim judges and intellectuals after independence. In his application form for study overseas in 1953, Wali's recommenders included Shaykh Awad Muhammad Ahmad, the Sudanese principal of NPLS/SAS from 1947 to 1959 and Northern Nigeria's first Grand Qadi from 1960 to 1962, as well as two Nigerians. The first was Aliyu Abubakar (1917 to ca. 1988), who would later serve as the first Nigerian Principal of SAS from 1959 to 1962, obtain a Ph.D. from the University of Cairo in 1967, and publish *Al-Thaqāfa al-'Arabiyya fī Nayjīriyā* (Arabic Culture in Nigeria), a text that both documented Nigeria's Islamic past and advocated a form of Islamic modernism. The second was Abubakar Gumi (1924–1992), who served as Nigeria's Deputy Grand Qadi under Awad from 1960 to 1962 and then as Grand Qadi from 1962 to 1967, as well as religious advisor to Northern Nigeria's Premier, Ahmadu Bello. Gumi would later become a virulent critic of Sufism, publishing the anti-Sufi polemic *Al-'Aqīda al-Ṣaḥīḥa bi-Muwāfaqat al-Sharī'a* (The Correct Creed in Accordance with the Law) in 1972 and becoming the spiritual patron of the anti-Sufi organization Jamā'at Izālat al-Bid'a wa-Iqāmat al-Sunna (The Society for Removing Blameworthy Innovation and Establishing the Prophet's Model, better known as Izala), which was founded in 1978. That Wali would be close to both Aliyu Abubakar and Abubakar Gumi in the 1940s and 1950s indicates the degree to which NPLS/SAS helped to incubate both Islamic modernism and anti-Sufism in Northern Nigeria.

In 1954, Wali became part of a cohort of Northern Nigerian Muslims sent to Sudan by the colonial administration. The logic that had propelled the importation of Sudanese teachers continued to guide this project: colonial administrators feared that Northern Nigerian Muslims were still too "rigid,"[33] and hoped that exposure to life in Sudan would give rising young Arabists and judges a more expansive worldview. Wali was sent, on his own, to study Arabic publishing at the University of Khartoum from 1954–55, as preparation for working at the Northern Regional Literature Agency (NORLA) on his return. In parallel, a group of six other NPLS graduates, including Gumi as well as Wali's future co-author Haliru Binji (1922–93), were sent to Sudan's Bakht-er-Ruda College to study Arabic. Yet another group, which included Aliyu Abubakar, was sent to study Arabic at London's School for Oriental and African Studies. These international trajectories were an additional ingredient in propelling Islamic modernism in Northern Nigeria: international exposure led young Northern Muslims to consider the triangular relationships among Northern Nigeria's classical Islamic heritage, European-style modernity, and their experiences in Arab lands.

Wali returned from Sudan to become director of NORLA from 1956 to 1959. NORLA was a government agency closely associated with the Gaskiya Corporation, which published the North's Hausa-language *Gaskiya Ta Fi Kwabo* newspaper, and was also associated with the Northern Regional government's literacy campaign Yaki da Jahilci (The War on Ignorance). The agency published dozens of books in English and Hausa between 1954 and 1960.[34] NORLA published texts by colonial officials,[35] as well as by Nigerian authors, especially graduates of colonial schools. Some of these texts encapsulated elements of the emerging Islamic modernism in Northern Nigeria. For example, Na'ibi's classmate and fellow returnee from Sudan, Haliru Binji, published a two-volume text called *Ibada da Hukunci a Addinin Musulunci* (Worship and Rulings in the Religion of Islam) with NORLA in 1957 and 1960. *Ibada da Hukunci* distilled a central text in the classical Mālikī legal curriculum into a paraphrased Hausa. This style was meant to be easily accessible to literate readers seeking a fast route to comprehension of Islamic law. By explaining and translating Arabic technical terms and by presenting the law as straightforward, *Ibada da Hukunci* represented a new step in the effort by NPLS/SAS graduates to challenge classical Muslim scholars.[36] While not explicitly modernist, *Ibada da Hukunci* was implicitly addressed to the new, literate Muslim professional who had neither the time nor the inclination to study Islam in the classical style.

In a similar vein, Binji and Wali would publish *Mu Koyi Ajami da Larabci* (Let's Learn Ajami and Arabic) in 1960 with NORLA's successor, the Gaskiya Corporation. This text, intended for schoolchildren, aimed to make literacy in Arabic and the Arabic-derived Ajami script accessible to a wider audience— again, implicitly suggesting that modernizing and streamlining the classical pedagogical model was possible and desirable.[37] This treatment of knowledge was a forerunner of Wali's explicit articulation of Islamic modernism in the 1970s.

Islamic modernism in Wali's writings

Wali's mature writings forcefully articulate an Islamic modernist ideology. Three of his works—*Tarbiyya Ga Mutum* (*Upbringing for Man*, 1959), *Duniya, Ina Za Ki da Mu?* (World, Where Are You Taking Us?, 1974), and *Mu Koma Kan Hanya* (Let Us Get Back on the Path, 1975—formed a trilogy of "messages" (Hausa singular: *sako*) to the Muslims of northern Nigeria. Intended as works of moral instruction, these books enjoin readers to develop the moral and intellectual traits necessary, in Wali's view, for Muslims to thrive *as Muslims* in the modern world.

Wali's prose compositions of the 1970s extended and developed the literary techniques and religious ideas that he and Haliru Binji used in the 1950s and place them in an even more international intellectual milieu. *Duniya* and *Mu Koma* included numerous micro-translations of Qur'anic verses and *aḥādīth*, typically unmediated by the invocation of any tafsir (Qur'anic exegesis). In terms of sources, Wali juxtaposed scriptural passages with quotations from both classical (e.g., Imam Abu al Hamid al-Ghazali) and twentieth-century thinkers (e.g., Shaykh Hassan al-Banna and Dr. Muhammad Qutb of the Egyptian Muslim Brotherhood).

Wali's writing was partly motivated by quintessentially Islamic modernist questions, which he framed within particular constructions of time. Depicting the past, including Nigeria's precolonial past, as a time of Muslim progress and achievement, and the present as a time of Muslim backwardness and European domination, he asked

> So, since things are this way, what has made Muslims today forget this teaching, and regress, and become followers, imitators? And the Europeans, too, who are not Muslims, have achieved progress, so that in the perception of the lazy, and the bewildered, no one can defeat them in this area? How have these surprising things happened?[38]

The problem, Wali answered, was internal to Muslims. Muslims had lost their way, he wrote, because they had abandoned their religion. The way forward necessitated a process of renewal, especially at the individual level. This renewal must focus partly on worldly change, and partly on preparation for salvation: "In Islam there is the world and the afterlife, not the world alone or the afterlife alone."[39]

Triangulating, Wali opposed his brand of Islamic modernism to two groups: irreligious modernists and traditionalist Muslims. Although hedonism seduces Westerners, he wrote, the traditionalists succumb to apathy. Echoing the 1943 speech at NPLS quoted above, Wali criticized forms of *tawakkal* (reliance on Allah) that had become, in his view, a pretext for laziness.

> I have brought forth all these explanations and pieces of advice so that one will not make excuses in the name of Allah and Religion, lazily saying, 'We Muslims, or ulama, or students, it is no concern of ours to waste time pursuing this worldly life.' Doing this kind of thinking is letting Satan—who wants to see the dignity of Muslims, ulama, and students erode—get the better of them.[40]

Of the two kinds of opponents he named, Wali devoted much more time to criticizing the traditionalists. Answering them required addressing their alleged belief that all modern inventions and industries are the province of unbelievers alone.

Muslims have become extremely ignorant of their religion, so that they have even taken the knowledge of crafts which Allah and the Prophet have commanded [us] to seek, and the earliest ulama have explained in detail, they have taken this kind of knowledge as "modern knowledge for Europeans" (*ilimin zamani ne na Turawa*), saying that because Europeans brought it, it is a hateful thing! [They say] for that reason it should be left to "pagans" (*arna*) to keep on doing it, and that Muslims should only pray and go on Hajj![41]

Wali rejected this perspective, arguing that pursuing knowledge of modern crafts was a communal religious obligation (*faralin kifaya*). "Knowledge," he wrote, "so long as it is united with religion, does not mislead people, or destroy them."[42]

Wali's endorsement of modern knowledge and technology coexisted with his fierce opposition to colonialism and what he calls neo-colonialism. Colonialism held Muslim countries back, he argued, and neo-colonialism continued to harm the progress of Muslim countries.[43] Modernism, however, was not synonymous with colonialism or the West. Knowledge could therefore be decoupled from colonialism.

In *Duniya*, Wali distinguished between the useful inheritances of European colonialism and its morally corrupting aspects. He saw some European systems as social goods: "Among [Europeans'] good customs are cleanliness for the body, clothing, and the residence, and also [their habit of] doing everything in the world systematically. They gave women respect. They have good principles for greeting each other and arranging meetings or celebrations and other matters."[44] Yet European modernity was also flawed. The Europeans had abandoned their religion (Christianity) and embraced a false ideology of "progress" (*cigaba*) based on two principles: that a man's value depends on the worldly wealth he accumulates, and that everyone is "liberated" (*sakakke*) to do as he pleases. They pursue worldly knowledge to the exclusion of spirituality.[45] Western modernity corrupted the morality of women, engendered selfishness, and promoted racial discrimination.[46] Some Muslims, Wali said, live under the spell of a neocolonialism that "controls hearts, brains, and thinking." They had caught this sickness. "These people you would only call monkeys: everything that Europeans do, they imitate."[47]

Critical to the articulation of Islamic neomodernism, in Wali's works, was his depiction of Islam in largely generic terms.[48] Although his periodic references to core Maliki texts gave his writings a Maliki frame, he avoided discussion of Sufi orders for either praise or blame. Instead, he opposed the modern to the traditional in broad terms. His definitions of religion and Islam emphasized not creedal purity, but moral development and action:

Religion is a creed (*akida*) that has complete influence over heart, mind, and body, as a result of which one has faith, follows a system, and works with it. The Muslim religion, then, is faith and following the laws and system that Allah has brought down to his followers by the hand of the Prophet Muhammad (Peace and Blessings

Upon Him) so that they may both work with it in their worldly lives and earn its result in the afterworld.[49]

Wali paired generic Islam with an ethic of spiritual development. He wrote, "Religious knowledge (*ilimin addini*) is correcting the character and educating the heart, by way of knowing Allah and working with His Command, and loving his followers and working to help them, because of seeking the blessing of Allah."[50] Proper "upbringing" was necessary to transmit the values that would produce such character. The final pages of *Mu Koma* listed five qualities that comprise *tarbiyya*, or moral education: *juriya* (endurance), *sadaukarwa* (dedication), *ladabi* (politeness), *kamun kai* (discipline), and *mancewa da kai* (forgetting about the self; i.e., dedicating oneself to Allah).

The individual who embraced these qualities, Wali suggested, would be able to pursue knowledge in an authentically Islamic fashion, and thereby reform society without imitating Europe's irreligious modernity or traditionalism's ignorant renunciation. Wali's Islamic modernism urged the individual to break free of tradition, hierarchy, and custom in the interest of leading the group forward. An intra-Muslim conflict over values was a necessary step toward reform in Wali's eyes, but this conflict was between modernity and tradition, not between different theological sects. The progressive moral individual will emerge victorious, he hoped, and become a systematizing influence in a disorderly society. Notably, this perspective entailed a substantial rejection of elements of Wali's own educational background, particularly the traditional context out of which his father had emerged and the colonial context in which he himself had been schooled.

Conclusion

Although this article has focused on Wali's intellectual trajectory through the 1970s, it is important to note that he remained an important player in the religious and political life of northern Nigeria until his death in 2013. He served as imam of the Umar Ibn Khattab Mosque of Kano, as member of numerous government committees and boards (including some associated with the shari'a implementation effort in Kano after 1999), and as chairman of Kano's Islamic Foundation. As mentioned above, Wali's brand of Islamic modernism did not translate into a social movement with a mass constituency, but his ideas have continued to resonate, including among younger intellectuals such as the poet and activist Aminu Sagagi.

Examining the trajectory of Northern Muslim elites from colonialism to the postcolonial period enriches understandings of how colonial education affected Muslim intellectuals. Previous scholarship on colonial Northern Nigeria has shown how, during the 1930s and 1940s, graduates of Western-style schools "reproduced and critically engaged" colonial discourses about Africa and Islam.[51] This article has examined such graduates at a later stage in their intellectual development. Wali, in his polemical writings during the 1970s, voiced a sharply anticolonial vision of Islamic modernism—reproducing some colonial discourses in his criticisms of traditional scholars, but attempting to break with colonial inheritances in his articulation of an Islamic modernity that would be fundamentally different from, and morally superior to, European-style modernity.

This seeming paradox—a graduate of colonial schools who becomes a critic of colonialism—fits within a broader pattern wherein colonial schooling produced unintended consequences. For example, in Ghana and Burkina Faso, graduates of Western-style schools became constituents for Muslim anti-Sufi reformist movements.[52] By observing graduates of colonial schools over the course of their lives and by analyzing their intellectual production at different points in their careers, we gain a rich sense of how their attitudes toward colonialism shifted over time. Wali sought not only to Islamize modernity, but to reject the colonial version of it—a maneuver that reflected Northern Nigerian elites' reappraisal of the colonial encounter in light of the political turbulence that affected Nigeria in the 1960s and 1970s. Wali also sought to reposition Islamic education as a force for moral renewal and spiritual decolonization. In doing so, he rejected both classical and colonial pedagogies.

Notes

1. Mass education in northern Nigeria has been an arena characterized by persistent experimentation and occasional conflict. Various colonial and postcolonial administrations have sought to domesticate Qur'an schools; on this, see Hannah Hoechner, *Searching for Recognition: Traditional Qur'anic Students (almajirai) in Kano, Nigeria* (Ibadan, Nigeria: IFRA-Nigeria, 2013). Meanwhile, faltering efforts to achieve universal primary enrollment have unwittingly spurred the growth of private schools; on this, see Muhammad S. Umar, "Education and Islamic Trends in Northern Nigeria: 1970s–1990s," *Africa Today* 48, no. 2 (2001): 127–50 and Mark Bray, *Universal Primary Education in Nigeria: A Study of Kano State* (Boston, MA: Routledge and Kegan Paul, 1981). Another trend has been the emergence of hybrid "Islamiyya" schools, blending secular and Islamic subjects. Such schools have been objects of political controversy; see Jonathan Reynolds, *The Time of Politics (Zamanin Siyasa): Islam and the Politics of Legitimacy in Northern Nigeria, 1950–1966* (San Francisco, CA: University Press of America, 2001); and, most notoriously, Western-style schooling has been denounced as un-Islamic by a vocal fringe, most notoriously the armed movement Boko Haram.
2. John Esposito and John Voll, *Makers of Contemporary Islam* (New York, NY: Oxford University Press, 2001), 3.
3. On the idea of "multiple modernities," see S. N. Eisenstadt, "Multiple Modernities," *Daedalus* 129 (2000): 1–29.
4. Marian Aguiar, *Tracking Modernity: India's Railway and the Culture of Mobility* (Minneapolis, MN: University of Minnesota Press, 2011).
5. Travis Cook, "Engineering Modernity: The Aswan Low Dam and Modernizing the Nile," Department of History Capstone Paper, Western Oregon University, 2013.

6. Charles Kurzman, "Introduction: The Modernist Islamic Movement," in *Modernist Islam, 1840–1940: A Sourcebook*, edited by Charles Kurzman (New York, NY: Oxford University Press, 2002), 3–27, 4.

7. See, for example, Albert Hourani, *Arabic Thought in the Liberal Age, 1798–1939* (Cambridge, UK: Cambridge University Press, 1983 [1962]).

8. Kurzman, "Introduction," 4.

9. Ibrahim Abu-Rabi', *Intellectual Origins of Islamic Resurgence in the Modern Arab World* (Albany, NY: SUNY Press, 1996), 9.

10. Indira Gesink, *Islamic Reform and Conservatism: Al-Azhar and the Evolution of Modern Sunni Islam* (London, UK: I.B. Tauris, 2014), 7.

11. David Commins, *Islamic Reform: Politics and Social Change in Late Ottoman Syria* (New York, NY: Oxford University Press, 1990), 142.

12. Muhammad Sani Umar, *Islam and Colonialism: Intellectual Responses of Muslims of Northern Nigeria to British Colonial Rule* (Leiden, The Netherlands: Brill, 2006), 157.

13. Umar, 2006, 158.

14. Quoted in Aliyu Abubakar, *Al-Thaqafa al-'Arabiyya fi Nayjiriya min 1804 ila 1960 'Am al-Istiqlal* (Beirut, Lebanon: no publisher, 1972), 345.

15. Alhaji Mahmood Yakubu, "Introduction: the Life of Sa'adu Zungur," in *Sa'adu Zungur: An Anthology of the Social and Political Writings of a Nigerian Nationalist*, edited by Alhaji Mahmood Yakubu (Kaduna: Nigerian Defence Academy Press, 1999), 1–108, 16.

16. Yakubu, 1999, 31.

17. Some sources list 1944 as the date of the Discussion Circle's founding.

18. Abubakar, 1972, 184.

19. Na'ibi Sulaiman Wali, *Mu Koma Kan Hanya* (Zaria, Nigeria: NNPC, 1975), 18.

20. Wali, 1975, 19.

21. Dandatti Abdulkadir, *The Poetry, Life, and Opinions of Sa'adu Zungur* (Zaria, Nigeria: NNPC, 1974), 100.

22. Abdulkadir, 1974, 77.

23. Abdulkadir, 1974, 81.

24. Abdulkadir, 1974, 89.

25. Abdulkadir, 1974, 95.

26. National Archives Kaduna (NAK) AN 251, "Naibi Sulaimanu Wali."

27. Ibid.

28. Alhaji Bala Sulaiman, "The Role of Shahuci and School for Arabic Studies, Kano, in the Development of Legal Education in Northern Nigeria to 1967" (MA Thesis in History, Bayero University Kano, Kano, Nigeria, 1990).

29. Sulaiman, 1990, 93.

30. Education Department, Nigeria, "Syllabus, School of Arabic Studies" (Zaria, Nigeria: Gaskiya Corporation, c. 1948), 3.

31. Abubakar Gumi with Ismaila Tsiga, *Where I Stand* (Ibadan, Nigeria: Spectrum Books, 1992), 64.

32. Umar, 2006, 215.

33. N. J. Brooke, *Report of the Native Courts (Northern Provinces) Commission of Inquiry* (Lagos, Nigeria: Government Printer, 1952), 121.

34. Ibrahim Yaro Yahaya, *Hausa a Rubuce: Tarihin Rubuce Rubuce Cikin Hausa* (Zaria: Kamfanin Buga Littattafai na Nigeria ta Arewa, 1988).

35. See, for example, J.G. Davies, *The Biu Book: A Collation and Reference Book on Biu Division* (Zaria, Nigeria: NORLA, 1954).

36. Haliru Binji, *Ibada da Hukunci a Addinin Musulunci*, Volume 1 (Zaria, Nigeria: NORLA, 1957).

37. Haliru Binji and Na'ibi Sulaiman Wali, *Mu Koyi Ajami da Larabci* (Zaria, Nigeria: Gaskiya Corporation, 1960).
38. Wali, 1960, 13.
39. Wali, 1960, 12.
40. Wali, 1960, 51.
41. Wali, 1960, 33–34.
42. Wali, 1960, 37.
43. Wali, 1960, 14.
44. Na'ibi Sulaiman Wali, *Duniya, Ina Za Ki da Mu?* (Zaria, Nigeria: NNPC, 1974), 10.
45. Wali, 1974, 8.
46. Wali, 1974, 10.
47. Wali, 1974, 8.
48. On the idea of "generic Islam," see Benjamin Soares, *Islam and the Prayer Economy: History and Authority in a Malian Town* (Ann Arbor, MI: University of Michigan Press, 2005), 224.
49. Wali, 1960, 7.
50. Wali, 1960, 29.
51. Umar, 2006, 215.
52. Ousman Kobo, *Unveiling Modernity in Twentieth-Century West African Islamic Reforms* (Leiden, the Netherlands: Brill, 2012).

Index

Note: Page numbers in bold and italics refer to table and figures.

www.ingramcontent.com/pod-product-compliance
Ingram Content Group UK Ltd.
Pitfield, Milton Keynes, MK11 3LW, UK
UKHW010021280225
455677UK00023B/724